Letters From A Cruiser

Letters From A Cruiser

Letters sent home by Laraine Salmon from 1988 to 1992 describing the circumnavigation she and her husband Mark completed in their sailboat "ARIETTA", a Standfast 36.

Laraine Salmon

iUniverse, Inc.
New York Lincoln Shanghai

Letters From A Cruiser

Letters sent home by Laraine Salmon from 1988 to 1992 describing the circumnavigation she and her husband Mark completed in their sailboat "ARIETTA", a Standfast 36.

iUniverse, Inc.

For information address:
iUniverse, Inc.
2021 Pine Lake Road, Suite 100
Lincoln, NE 68512
www.iuniverse.com

ISBN: 0-595-27972-4

Printed in the United States of America

Contents

Letter 1
Getting Started

It has been six months since we left our familiar sailing area in Northern California and headed for the warmer waters of the south. Still holding the uncontested title of "Worlds Worst Correspondent" I am trying, in this letter, to catch up. Although I am sure some of you hate writing as much as I do perhaps you could manage an occasional note. It would be much appreciated! Any news or gossip from home would be great.

Our trip, which we planned for so very long, began Saturday, August 13, 1988 when we sailed out, across a racing fleet, under the Golden Gate Bridge in moderate winds and very sloppy seas.

The trip down the coast of California was one of day sailing from one familiar anchorage to the next, or more frequently than we would have wished, motor sailing, since the winds were unusually light and frequently from the south. We rounded the infamous Pt Conception in calm seas with the spinnaker flying. I will mention now that the spinnakers have been our most heavily used headsails, especially along the Mexican mainland coast and have often been the difference between sailing and motoring. The only problem with a spinnaker, and a crew of two is that you must be careful to get it down early if the wind is building.

From Pt Conception we sailed to San Miguel Island passing an oilrig—Sedco 712—on which Mark did major design work three years ago while working for a firm that designed off shore oil drilling rigs. I received a most interesting and informative lecture on the workings of a semi-submersible exploration-drilling rig. At least I smiled politely and tried to appear to be extremely interested.

Having begun this trip as totally incompetent fishermen we didn't catch any fish for a while. Our first, a rockfish at San Miguel, turned out to be of a type impossible not to catch, and hardly a fisherman's delight. However we were very excited to have landed it—our first catch. I'm sure we made a comical picture, Mark in the dingy with the fish, a knife and the cutting board, and me on the boat, reading from our fishing cookbook the step-by-step instruction on how to filet a fresh fish. What innocents we were.

We spent Aug 25 to Oct 13 in the California Channel Islands with a brief visit to Santa Barbara for fresh water and a few provisions.

The serenity of San Miguel, Santa Rosa, Santa Cruz, Santa Barbara and Anacapa Islands gave us a wonderful opportunity to learn, and at least attempt to accustom ourselves to a certain measure of self-sufficiency.

Mark snorkeled for hours every day and learned to use his spear gun. Although the water was cold he did fine with the short wet suit and provided countless meals of fresh fish. He is an excellent swimmer; easily free diving to 30 feet.

My project was getting Morse code to 13 wpm so I could complete my General Class Ham Radio license exam in San Diego. It was not easy for me, and I struggled with is and sometimes found myself, at night, dreaming in Morse code—frightening thought, isn't it!

Of all the Channel Islands I liked Santa Barbara Island best. Seals are protected in California and have been for many seal generations. Consequently they have gotten over their fear of man, since the days when they were slaughtered relentlessly for their pelts. The Santa Barbara's seals were most inquisitive and seemed to enjoy checking out the visitors. They would swim right up to the boat and peer at us as if to say "What do you want here?" One tiny one kept rubbing up to the dinghy and actually seemed to like having its head scratched. Mark loved diving and swimming among the seals in the beautiful Kelp forests growing profusely not far from our anchorage.

The other island, which fascinated me, mainly because of the ranger we met, was the tiny island of Anacapa. The ranger there was a woman who lives alone on the island. She showed us around and told us that Anacapa was a huge seagull nesting ground. She showed us all the 'garbage', such as the leftover chicken bones, that the adults would fly in from the mainland to feed their young. Seagull chicks gain their adult size in about 6 weeks, but still chirp and act like chicks, so the adults are kept frantic tying to feed their rapidly growing youngsters. Gaining their adult size so quickly is the result of being ground nesters. If they do not get large they will not be able to survive a myriad of predators who can reach them easily on the ground. I found the idea of a woman living alone on this isolated island a bit of a survival story as well. You would have to be a person very contented with your own company for long periods of time to get by without suffering unbearable loneliness.

Having anchored everywhere since leaving S.F. we decided to dig into the cruising kitty and pay for a mooring in Avalon Harbor. I expected Catalina to be a shock after the desolation and solitude of the other islands, and it was, but in spite of its obvious emphasis on the tourist trade it was delightfully charming and I loved it. I also loved a luxurious meal, ashore, in a restaurant. The first I had not cooked myself in 2 months, but we were celebrating our 5th Wedding anniversary, so it gave us an excuse to splurge.

In San Diego we spent time with friends, my parents visited, I managed to pass the Morse Code exam and get my General Class Ham License and we installed a small refrigeration unit. After drinking warm beer for 3 month Mark decided the extra cost of a refrigerator was worth it. Later, as we became more competent fishermen, we were glad we had made this decision. After stocking up on food and spare parts, and after a brief overnight stay in Encinada we set off on the first long sail of the trip.

Anxious to get to warm weather we decided not to stop anywhere until we got to Cabo San Lucus, provided the wind held. It was 5 days of wonderful sailing and Marks longest non-stop ever. I had cruised the coast of Baja in a previous visit many years before and since anything we experienced was new to Mark he didn't mind getting to warmer waters ASAP. We tried out our trolling generator, a 'Mark' aka Rube Goldberg design, and it put out 5 amps, 24 hours a day, for 5 days.

Cabo, when we arrived, was very hot and the water was like bath water, but the cooler weather was moving in quickly. The town had grown considerably since I had cruised there last in 1971 and the anchorage situation has changed considerably since the disastrous storm in 1982. The sheltered area, where breaking waves did the most damage in 82, is all set with moorings, mostly occupied by sport fishing boats. That means that the free anchorage area is a considerable dingy ride to the harbor. The inner harbor, on the other hand, was far too dirty for swimming, even thought more convenient. We preferred the swimming and used the dingy for the long ride to town.

One thing we found about cruising is that you have time for people. Other cruisers we have met all seem so friendly, but it is because you have the time to be. If you want to spend 2 or 3 hours in the middle of the day chatting, why not? You have time to get acquainted without the pressures of the 8 to 5 rat race, and all that it entails. Friendships blossom beautifully in this climate.

From Cabo, although it is not the time of year to do so, we went into the Sea of Cortez. It was cooling down rapidly, but we are not planning to be back this way and wanted to at least have a glimpse of the area. Perhaps someday we will spend time here, but staying in Mexico an extra year in order to be in the Sea of Cortez for the summer is not something we are prepared to do just now.

The passage to the mainland was another fantastic sail, averaging well over the required 6 knots needed to arrive in daylight.

Between Mazatlan and Banderas Bay there is a bird sanctuary. Isla Isabella is a delight to visit. The Brown Boobies, Blue Footed Boobies and Frigate Birds are not threatened by any enemies and seem almost unafraid of human visitors. The Boobies nest on the ground and we were able to get close enough to see the young chicks clearly, without frightening them. Like seagulls they grow to full adult size very rapidly. They retain their soft fluffy white down coats and are quite helpless, but totally adorable. The frigate birds are rather fascinating. Highly aerial, they cannot swim, but live on fish, cannot walk, so they nest in trees. Their shriveled feet are only good for gripping branches. In the air they are a joy to watch, gliding high above the islands with no motion, just a slight flap of wings when they wish to change direction, swooping down to skim inches above the waters surface and pluck a fish from the sea with effortless grace. They are also notorious thieves, grabbing food from the more clumsy Boobies and slower, beautiful, Tropic Birds.

Had we not arranged to pick up mail in Puerto Vallarta I think we would have just as well skipped it. The charm it had, made famous by the Movie 'The Sand-pipers' has been destroyed by over development. It is dirty, overcrowded and the water is filthy. No swimming in this polluted harbor.

The one thing about Banderas Bay that was really exciting, were the whales. It is a breading ground for them and they come in large numbers all the way from Alaska each winter. There were several that came close to us, almost too close for comfort and it was quite an experience to see them all at that close range. I must say though, that if you are down wind when they blow you realize that dental hygiene is totally lacking, and their diet is mainly fish. They suffer from acute halitosis.

The strip of the coast from Banderas Bay to Manzanillo is a lazy cruiser's dream. Day sails between beautiful anchorages, fish in abundance, bathing suits for foul weather gear and wonderful spinnaker weather.

Our fishing prowess has increased considerably since that first fishing in the Channel Islands and since we both like to eat fish it certainly is an improvement over canned anything. They are abundant in this area. I have one fish story I must tell you, which in retrospect we laugh about. We always tow a line when we are underway in daylight and if we get a fish my first job is to run below and close the little ports in the cockpit by the quarter berths to avoid having any fish blood splash through them onto the bunks. Leaving Bahia Navidad we caught a huge Dorado (Mahi Mahi). We had quite a difficult time landing him since he was so big. He leapt straight out of the water repeatedly trying franticly to shake the hook and was a beautiful sight to see. We finally landed him and he was huge. He thrashed wildly on board and to our utter horror propelled himself through the hatchway and into the cabin where he thrashed about even more franticly beating himself on the cabin floor, the table and the settees. We were in shock for a moment, staring, mouths agape in disbelief at the mess. Mark recovered sufficiently to grab a winch handle and a glove and go below to grab him, toss him back up into the cockpit, and finally do him in. Luckily the settee cushions are fabric on one side and vinyl on the other and when we are underway the vinyl side is up. Everything else is varnished so the clean up was a chore, but no permanent damage was done. When we measured him he was 48 inches from his nose to the V in his tail. We ate well for quite a while after that catch. Mahi Mahi is just about my favorite fish and is delicious no matter how you fix it. We revised our routine for hauling in fish to include putting in a hatch board as well as closing the ports.

Items overboard can be a source of interesting stories—also in retrospect. One took place when Mark's shoe, tied loosely, caught on a cleat, pulled off his foot, and threw itself in to the sea. Of course this happened right in the middle of a spinnaker jibe. It is a bit hard to change direction when the shoot is free flying because someone is more interested in his shoe than connecting the pole. Surprisingly we actually did manage to recover the shoe, but only because it floated very well. After dousing the shoot and backtracking we managed to snag it with the boat hook. Another item overboard occurred when I was hanging out a wet bathing suit on the lifeline to dry. The top fell in the drink and it did not float. A couple of attempts to grab it with the boat hook failed and it was sinking fast. On the next pass it was just a blob below the water and I was resigned to its loss. Suddenly I heard a splash and saw Mark dive into the water. It seemed like ages before he surfaced with a big grin holding up the errant bathing suit top. I just missed snagging a 170lb Salmon named Mark on the trailing fishing line. I did manage to recover him, after he decided that his being in the water and my being on the helm was not the time to tell me how to run a boat. I did teach him to sail after all. So when he quieted down with the orders I decided not to make him swim the 5 miles to shore and recovered both Mark and the bathing suit. Of course I could not help delivering a lecture on the dangers of going overboard at sea, but after that excitement we continued on our way. It had been a hot day, and I guess a swim seemed inviting and he is a good swimmer, but, fortunately for him, I like him and want to keep him. Otherwise it would have made a good plot for a disappearing husband story since it is a long way to swim to the Mexican coast.

The sailing from Manzanillo to Zihuatanejo has not been very exciting. The winds get lighter and lighter and the need to motor in order to get anywhere is more frequent, so this will probably be our last stop in Mexico. Mark looks forward to his first ocean crossing and I am excited about revisiting the South Pacific. The Marquesas beckon. So far the trip has been a success in that we have had no major gear failures and we are managing a high level of self-sufficiency. All the years of dreaming and planning are paying off and we are meeting some wonderful new friends. Life is good! Hoping to hear from you. Laraine

Letter 2
Mexico to the Marquesas

We arrived on the island of Hiva Oa about 8:00 am March 31st, after a 24-day passage from Zihuatanejo Mexico. Hiva Oa is the administrative center for the Southern Marquesas. When I was here before I did not visit the Southern Marquesas only the Northern Islands of Nuka Hiva and Ua Pou, so we decided to start at the southern part this time as they are harder to sail to once you are in the northern group, being straight upwind. From Hiva Oa, we will sail upwind to Fatu Hiva about 40 miles, but that is unavoidable. You are not supposed to go to Fatu Hiva until you have checked in at Hiva Oa or we would have gone there first, and avoided beating to weather altogether. However, being good upstanding citizens not wanting to get into trouble with the French Gendarmes we came here first and got the visa red tape out of the way. On the passage from Mexico Mark had worked very hard with his French language tapes to be prepared. Of course we had just come from Mexico where we had struggled to speak some Spanish. Mark was doing quite well with French when we were checking in, but as we were leaving the office, relaxing a bit after trying so hard he casually thanked the officer saying 'Gracias'. Everyone laughed and I suspect he is not the first to have made this linguistic slip.

The French allow you a 3-month visa to begin with. This can be extended, but only if you apply to Papeete. They also require that you post a bond, which amounts to leaving a sum of money on deposit with them, which is totally refundable, when you leave French Polynesia. This deposit is supposed to be sufficient to cover your airfare to an American port if they want you out of their country. For each of us it was $850.00 U.S. dollars. Of course, it is much more expensive for non-Americans, since Hawaii is quite a convenient distance from French Polynesia. If you are a Canadian, it is about $1600.00 U.S. dollars to cover the airfare back to Canada. Of course, if you are from somewhere like England, it would be very expensive, since it is a long air flight. For us, just 2 people, it isn't too bad. We paid in travelers-checks, and you aren't getting any interest on your travelers' check dollars anyway, so it isn't a great inconvenience. One

Canadian boat we talked to had money transferred from their Canadian bank, where it was earning interest. They had to come up with an amount sufficient to cover 2 adults, as well as several teenage children. Children under 12 are only ½ price, which helps a bit for large families. I can understand the reasoning of the French, however, since they don't want a bunch of freeloaders littering their islands. When a yacht arrives with several extra crewmembers, it has been known for crew to jump ship and "live off the land".

Atuona, the main town on Hiva Oa has a tiny bank, a hardware store and a couple of grocery stores. There is a French Foreign Legion base, which, we found out from one of the Legionnaires, is mainly an R&R base. The town's main claim-to-fame is that the artist, Paul Gauguin is buried here.

The island itself, like all the Marguesan Islands, is volcanic in origin. The mountains rise straight up and are quite spectacular to see. Because of the huge amount of rain, almost anything will grow here. It is odd that you cannot buy fruit, or vegetables in the grocery stores, until you realize that everyone just has their own in their yard, or near their house. At first we were anxious to have all the wonderful fresh fruit, especially after being at sea, and we couldn't buy it. We had an occasional breadfruit, or pomplamous (grapefruit-like fruit) or mango given to us, but it took us a week to locate a fellow who actually does actively farm and sell his produce (probably to the French Legionnaires). We now have a good supply of cucumber, cantaloupe, pomplamous, oranges, bananas, avocados, sweet potatoes, and mangos. The mangos are wonderful! Imagine a taste some-how combining a mango, an apple and a bowl of honey. I cannot really describe their flavor, but they are so good that a person like me who used to hate mangos cannot get enough of them. And I have yet to find one that is stringy. All butter smooth and melt in the mouth. As far as other supplies are concerned with a few exceptions like flour and canned butter, which are subsidized, the prices are very high. We are glad we stocked up well in Mexico

We have arrived at the tail end of the rainy season, and it is still wet. We put up the awning we made before we left home as an at anchor sun awning—totally needed in the tropics if you don't want to fry. It has side panels you can roll down to catch rainwater and we totally filled all our water tanks in one torrential down-pour. Sure beats carting jerry jugs back and forth from shore in the dinghy.

The harbor here is not too nice, from the standpoint of swimming that is. The water is muddy, since there is a very large stream emptying into it and we have been told there are a lot of sharks, which, although not too large, are not too friendly. Ashore, however, they have built a shower and laundry tub for anyone to use, with unlimited amounts of water, so this compensates for not being able to swim. It is very hot and humid (end of summer). It is tempting to jump in the water but, since this is one of the few places like this (muddy water), we will wait. Once we leave Atuona, we will be able to jump in and cool off just about anywhere else we visit.

This place is a pleasure to visit. Everyone is so nice. If you are walking to town (3 kilometers), almost anyone will stop and give you a ride and people just seem to like people. Perhaps, it is because life is easy here. Food is plentiful, and housing is easy to construct, with no need for heating. Whatever the reason they are most cordial. You ask where something is, and they take you there. Very accommodating!

As for the trip here, now that we are here, it seems like it was over very quickly. Of the boats that we were in contact with, by radio on the way, we had the fastest passage. We attacked the trip like it was a race. We played a game all the way, pretending we were racing and marked our place each morning, against all our competitors, as you would in a race. Having been avid racers in the Bay Area it is hard not to play at racing. We left from Zihuatanejo and most of the others left from Manzanillo, which is actually 80 miles closer to the Marquesas but we were 24-days and the next was 27. Of course I am sure that is not in any way a record since it was a very light air trip. Some days, we were almost totally becalmed and light air sailing can be so frustrating trying to keep the sails even partial full. Each swell rolls the wind out of the sail and the sails flog terribly, but you just keep at it, and eventually get here. The worst part was a large area of "moist, unstable air", where there were huge thunderstorms. Lightening is one thing that frightens me, almost to death, aboard a sailboat. We were never actually in the lightening, but far closer than either of us would have liked to have been. These storms, although, not carrying huge amount of wind, covered the horizon from one side to the other, they were impossible to avoid, but at least the ones we were actually caught in were not too active. We came close to one two days out of here, which had us both on edge for several hours. I have never seen so much lightening in my life. It would have been quite beautiful to watch under different circumstances. In the end though we arrived safely, so that is all that matters

Again, one thing we were grateful for on this trip was that we had spinnakers in our sail inventory. They are absolutely necessary if you want to move in light air. One of our friends had one only, but it was a 1-½ oz, which is what our small one is, and he couldn't use it much because it would collapse in the same wind, in which our ¾ oz would fly. It meant we could sail when others were forced to turn on the engine if they wanted to make any progress at all.

We had one spinnaker wrap on the head stay, which sent Mark aloft to unwrap and made me wonder about making up some sort of a triangle "ladder" to hoist in the fore triangle to prevent this. Would probably be easy but would take a lot of line. It was actually quite exciting, as it happened just as a squall hit. There again—no damage.

My basic feeling about long ocean passages is the same as it was before we left Mexico. I love being out there, no matter that it did involve lightening, the one thing I truly did fear, but basically I loved the trip. Being in the ocean away from land, gives you a rare feeling of freedom. Granted, sailing a boat across an ocean requires a certain element of discipline, but it is self-inflicted and that, in itself, represents a form of freedom. A self-sufficiency rare in our world today.

The biggest problem I have in the Marquesas is the famous No-Nos. I am allergic to their bites. Every one comes up in a blister, so my favorite cologne these days is REI's Jungle Juice Bug Repellent. As long as I cover myself in it, I am ok. Mark, on the other hand, gets bit, scratches for a minute, then that is the end of it. Someone told me to eat lots of garlic, someone else said, "take Brewers Yeast". Luckily, I have lots of Jungle Juice.

Mark amazes me with his linguistic abilities. We both took the same Spanish class, but he could talk to the Mexican officials and find out the information needed, while I stood there like a dummy. Now, even though he modestly denied that he knows French very well, he can converse with the Marquesans well enough to discuss their attitudes toward the French and talk about the testing in the Tuamotoes, as well as how heavily taxed American goods are, as opposed to French items. All the Marquesans drive Land Rovers, which seem to hold up very well in this climate, and on their unbelievable roads—straight up—straight down—and lumpy. Mark asked why they didn't drive French vehicles, instead of British, and they told him the French were not tough enough for their roads.

I am anxious to get away from Atuona and visit some of the more remote villages, where there are no ships coming in with visitors and less French influence. The tourists who visit the Marquesas are the yachties, and a few who fly in aboard French military planes, or arrive on the inter-island supply ships. So, it is a far removed scene from the average tourist resort, and not set up for tourist at all. They don't even sell post cards. However, for the Marquesas, Atuona is a major center with a dock for the supply boat and a landing strip for planes. There are so many places to go, both here in the Marquesas, and then the Tuamotoes and Societies and really so little time. Six months does not seem like much for such a large fascinating area, but that is all we are allowed. We have barely started. One week in Atuona is hardly a beginning, but it has been a good full week and after catching our breath, restocking with fresh fruits, veggies, and water, we are ready to head out. Our next stop is probably Fatu Hiva, then other places on Hiva Oa, when we come back this way, enroute to the Northern Marquesas.

The boat has been good. So far, we have not had any problems with gear breaking, or failure of any kind worth mentioning, which is wonderful. Of course this could change at any time, I suppose, but for now we are grateful we have a strong boat. We both think our perfect boat would have a 30-foot exterior, with a 50-foot interior, but until someone builds it, we like what we have. It certainly does sail well.

Guess that's all for now.

Laraine

Letter 3
Marquesas

Writing this in Toau. It is in the Tuamotoes the chain of atolls between the Marquesas and the Societies. Toau is one of the less populated of the atolls with only 12 people who live here full time. (Occasionally, there are more, temporarily, to harvest copra). This is the third atoll we have visited. Makemo, Kauehi, and Toau; the pronunciation is actually very simple. Sound out every letter; none are silent, and try not to accent any one more than another. Since there was no written language, until the missionaries came, they simply wrote words, spoken by the inhabitants, phonetically.

I will back track a little here since I don't think I told you much about the Marquesas. We visited four islands: Hiva Oa, Fatu Hiva, Tahuatu, and Ua Pou. We were a bit unlucky with weather, while we were there. It rained a great deal and the winds were very strong, making some of the anchorages extremely uncomfortable. The most spectacularly beautiful anchorage we have ever been in was Hanavave, and I would have loved to stay longer. When we sailed in I looked at it and thought it was too perfect to be natural and must have been designed and built by some Hollywood set designer and landscape artist. It is just breathtaking. Unfortunately it was just too wild an anchorage to be comfortable. It was windy, (40–45 knot gusts), and rainy and after watching one boat drag and another snap their stern anchor line, we decided to move on. In several of the places we anchored, we would have gone ashore but the surf was such that it was impossible to beach the inflatable dingy. When we did go ashore, I had to smother myself in Jungle Juice and wear long pants and long sleeve blouses to fight off the No-No's. (A bit uncomfortable in the hot, steamy weather we were having). It may sound as if I am complaining, but I don't mean to be. We actually enjoyed our stay tremendously and had some wonderful experiences. We met an extremely friendly Marquesan in Ua Pou (the head master of the junior school, on Easter vacation) who entertained us, along with two other couples, royally. He took us on a tour of the archeological sites at the old King's city, which at one time had a population of 3,000. Now, only one family lives there.

He and his wife had us for a wonderful meal, and the following day invited us for an evening of music (just a few friends with guitar and ukuleles, but fascinating) and finally a lunch, the day we left, of sashimi. Such warm hospitality is rare and most sincerely appreciated by this cruiser to be sure. Something else we enjoyed in the Marquesas were all the good fresh fruits. I just couldn't eat enough of them, especially the mangos.

Considering the history of the islands I find it amazing that the local people are so friendly and kind to us. At one time there were 100,000 Marquesans but due to Westerners and our murder, taking of slaves, and diseases, that population was reduced to 2000 at its lowest. It is back up to about 6,000 now, but still far from their former glory days. One fellow on Hiva Oa gave a huge slice of fresh, wild goat meat to our friends on the vessel "Hamelyn" and since they have no refrigeration they invited us to join them for a wonderful meal. It was delicious. She did it in onions and garlic and simmered it for about 1 1/4 hours then served it over rice.

The swimming in the Marquesas was not great because all the rain made the water in the anchorages very muddy, but the spectacular scenery more than compensated. It is breathtaking. It was a place I will never forget.

Our sail to the Tuamotoes was pleasant and uneventful. Uneventful passages are the best. The only problem is that you do not want to get too close in the dark so the last 12 hours we were trying to sail slowly. This is a very odd sensation; opposite to what you enjoy doing. We tried to time our arrival for slack water in the pass since at max ebb you can have up to 8 knots of current. Since our top motoring speed is 6 knots this would not work out too well. We actually timed it perfectly and went through just at the very start of the ebb with no mishaps. We anchored by the village the first two days and then found a totally isolated little reef, inside the atoll. Since we were the only sailboat in the whole atoll the feeling of solitude was delightful, and rare. We snorkeled some but I was a bit spooked by the sharks. They are small black tip reef sharks and I have gotten quite used to them now, but then I was afraid to stay in the water when I'd see one. Actually the first time I saw one I almost walked on water trying to get back into the dingy. Not knowing anything about the fish in the area we didn't spear or try to catch any but later found out that all the fish at Makemo are OK to eat. In some of the atolls there is a problem with eating fish due to a poison they can carry which causes serious neurological and nerve damage, but apparently this was not the case in Makemo. Better safe than sorry, however, if you do not have some local knowledge. At Kauehi we met "Out a Here" and "Cannibal". Two boats we had spoken to on the radio but had never met. Also, the boat "Mistral" which we met in Atuona. A funny thing about talking to people on the radio. You hear their voice and form a complete mental picture of them, but they never end up looking the way you expect. Like the radio announcer back home. In Kauehi we did find out which fish are OK to eat and ate a lots of them. Fish has always been one of my favorite foods. We went to a church service mainly to hear the music. The Polynesian voices and spontaneous (unaccompanied) harmonies are unbelievably beautiful. I just wish I'd a way to record it. The folks on "Cannibal" went and collected tern eggs with a local family and were generous enough to share them with us. They are about 1/3 smaller than our common hens eggs and actually taste quite similar but the strange thing to get use to is the color of the yoke—bright reddish orange. If you make scrambled eggs it looks like you've already added ketchup.

Going from Kauehi to Toau we caught a huge Mahi Mahi—51 inches. You can cook it any way—BBQ, fry, poach, broil—anything, and it is always wonderful eating.

Will say bye for now

Love from Laraine

Letter 4
Tuamotoes

The anchorage at Toau was the best of all. It was well protected from anything but a SW wind, which would be rare and we met two of the local people who made our stay there wonderfully unique. Mark's linguistic abilities, being able to speak French, was invaluable. Even though not fluent he was able to make conversation on a rather sophisticated level discussing views of life as well as basic pleasantries. We spent 4 weeks in Toau and we did so many things it is hard to list them all, but I will try to remember. We sampled a multitude of local food, which we would never have had the chance to try if we had not become so friendly and been able to communicate with Francois and Rauita. Both were born in the Tuamotoes but had left for many years, Rauita lived in France for a while. They have now been back in Toau for 3 years.

Although coconuts grow easily, if left to themselves, the brush that grows under and around them makes it impossible to harvest copra (coconuts) so they have been tearing it out, piece by piece, by hand. Coconuts come in male and female and the females produce the coconuts so they tear down most of the male trees and replace them with female trees. All this is hard work but they have done an amazing amount of work since they arrived with only the clothes on their back, a machete, a spear gun and their cooking pots. They have constructed traps for fish near the pass and when the copra boat comes they sell their fish, lobsters caught on the reef and copra. If they can get together the money for refrigeration they could do much better because they could stock pile the fish. Unfortunately, that requires expensive solar panel hook ups, since there is no electricity in Toau. While there, Mark spent 2 nights helping collect lobster and a day helping to spear fish for Francois to sell to the copra boat. Although, by American standards they are dreadfully poor, you would never know it by the generous, warm hospitality shown to us. Almost every night we got together for a visit. One day they took us on a trip to see a special coconut tree. There are actually 7 trees growing from one coconut—quite rate. We also went on an expedition to catch some blue-shelled crab, another delicacy. One day we went fishing by the passage in the reef and Francois taught us that you do not play the fish here, near the reef, because if you hesitate at all in landing them the sharks get their lunch. Rauita also told us the name of our boat "Arietta" is a common woman's name in this area and means a small cloud passing slowly overhead. Leaving after 4 weeks was a sad occasion, not without tears, as Rauita and I parted company.

From Toau we made a quick trip to Fakarava to say hello to Manihi Salmon. He told us that in about 1812 a family named Salmon came from England to French Polynesia and there are now hundreds of families with that name here. Manihi speaks fluent English having lived in New Zealand and Fiji and we had a pleasant conversation over coffee and signed his guest book of visiting yachts.

Now on to Papeete, the "big city", to re-provision although from what we have heard of costs it may just be for the bare necessities. It will be a complete change of pace. Will tell you all about it—next time.

Bye for now. Laraine

Letter 5
Society Islands and Tonga

Reluctantly, leaving the Tuamotoes we were Papeete bound, needing to fill up on propane, diesel, gasoline, and water. Contrary to some misconceptions, tourism is not one of the mainstays of the economy of Tahiti. In all of French Polynesia there are approximately the same number of hotel rooms as in one large hotel on Waikiki and the annual number of tourists is approx. the same as visit Disneyland during one busy weekend. It is grossly expensive and a real disappointment in some ways. The snorkeling in the reef surrounding Tahiti is not too good, especially if you have just come from the Tuamotoes. Most of the reefs are dead and the largest fish are about 3 inches. They have been seriously over fished. The restaurants unfortunately were too pricey for our cruising budget—a serious disappointment, since just reading the menus made my mouth water. On the bright side, the bread is delicious, the French butter and wine marvelous and N.Z. cheese quite inexpensive. So, calories, alcohol, carbs and cholesterol make a delicious lunch. The N.Z. frozen lamb is also very affordable but the local produce is expensive. Go figure!

We enjoyed Bora Bora best of all the Society Islands. A good place to ride bicycles and socialize at the Oa Oa Hotel. The road around the island has just a few hills that are of any challenge and you can go all the way around the island in half a day. Taking a picnic and lots of water is suggested. We had bicycles on board, but they were readily available for rent at some of the resorts. The anchorages in Bora Bora were mostly very easy and comfortable and the swimming absolutely lovely.

The next stop was the Tongan Vavau Island Group. Cruising is a constant serious of surprises, but what amazed me most about Tonga is how tiny it is. Since it is an independent monarchy you expect more of it somehow, but it is little. It is also very poor. However, it was interesting being in a country that has never been a colony. Somehow it seemed more authentically Polynesian. When we arrived it was the southern hemisphere's tropical mid-winter—August—and the temperature was actually quite cool in the evening. In the water wearing a

17

light wet suits made the swimming comfortable—the water being noticeably cooler than in Bora Bora. Beach combing, shelling, and relaxing is about all to do in Vavau. Totally, delightfully, relaxing. Few material items are available so re-provisioning is not practical. The few items that are available are reasonably priced and seem downright dirt-cheap after Fr. Polynesia. Handcrafts, especially woven baskets are beautifully made and a bargain. There was a restaurant in Niafu, 'Gunter's Belle Vue', our first dinner out since Mexico, which was an amazing surprise. Not very expensive and absolutely world-class quality. It was quite unexpected in this location. It would stand up to anything San Francisco has to offer. Gunter is an Austrian chef, who came here on vacation, met and fell in love with a local lady, got married and never left. The restaurant was so good that even on our tight cruising budget we simply could not resist going back a second time. The Apple Strudel was to die for. Within an area 10 miles by 10 miles you have the choice of about 40 anchorages and an equal number of islands. The "Moorings" Charter group has a fleet here both crewed and bare boats available and it seems a perfect place to charter a yachting vacation. One comical note in passing. The Moorings charter group puts out a map of various anchorages in this area. Each anchorage is numbered and described, and almost every cruiser manages to get hold of a copy of this Guide. It is the only place I have ever heard cruisers talking on the radio saying that they would meet tomorrow in anchorage number such and such. A lot of the numbers are adjacent to Tongan villages and if you go ashore children, friendly and rambunctious, inundate you. They holler "Palangi, palangi, palangi" what we referred to as the Palangi alert. Of course it means a westerner, or foreigner and with that alarm having been given the adults come out and visit. Frequently the women will have baskets or hats woven from palm fronds or beautiful tapa cloths to sell. We purchased several I will treasure when I am back home in the Bay area. If I am ever in the market for a charter vacation in the future Tonga is a place I would certainly keep in mind. I loved the snorkeling and shelling and collected some lovely shells that I will always treasure.

Next stop Fiji. In this case the reality has been a total surprise as to how extensive the area is. You could spend a very long time here. About <u>400</u> islands! We have 2 months, not nearly enough.

Suva is intriguing. The Fijian people are actually Melanesian, not Polynesian, and are their features more Negroid. They are an extremely handsome people with the young women being very stylish. But, oddly enough, the majority of the population is Indian. Indians were brought in early in the last century to work in the sugar cane fields and most of them stayed. Although the majority they are treated as second class citizens, and restricted in land ownership. But being very industrious, hard working and ambitious they have excelled at business and technical jobs they have been forced into. Although there have been times of turmoil and it could always be a problem, when there you are impressed with how easily the two groups mingle. Although intermarriage is rare just the fact that two such diverse groups could share the same islands if a hopeful sign for Fiji's future. The people in Suva smile easily, which is not always the case in cities. People seem to like each other. As with any big city you do have a certain amount of crime. Some boats in the harbor have been broken into, but compared to any city in America it is pretty safe. Would you leave a boat unlocked in any marina at home? Perhaps our stay in Fiji will seem too short. Some people do sit out the hurricane season here but it is risky, so we will definitely end up heading to N.Z. Right now though we are ready to investigate as much of Fiji as we can in two months. Tell you all about it in the next letter.

Bye for now,

Laraine

P.S. To those who have written, thanks. It may take a little time for our mail to catch up with us, but when it does we enjoy it so much. So, please write when you can. News from home is always a treat.

Letter 6
Fiji & New Zealand

Fiji was a joy to cruise. In two months however we merely scratched the surface. There are over 400 islands in all of the Fiji Groups so you could spend years here if you just had the time. We didn't, but had a good sample and enjoyed what we saw. Because of the recent coup the tourist industry has dropped off and the radio is full of advertisements telling the local people to be nice to tourists and impressing upon them the economic advantages of having tourist visit them. Other than theft in the Suva Harbor (a risk in any large urban area) we found the people almost overwhelmingly friendly. We actually found ourselves looking for anchorages away from the villages to ensure a little peace and privacy. All water in Fiji is "owned". In other words, you must get permission from the local village chief to anchor in his area. Taking a gift of yangona (known as kava kava), to the chief of each area you enter is the traditional way to introduce yourself and pay respects to his authority. It sounds like a bit of a bother but actually is quite fun. Some villages just accept your gift and say fine, thank you, now you can stay, visit, snorkel, fish, beachcomber, and enjoy your visit. Other villages, where they get fewer visitors, make a big fuss over you. They invite you to bring your gift and present it formally to the village elders. Then you are invited to share the Kava drinking ceremony, and frequently invited to lunch, or dinner, or in one case a fish BBQ on the beach. Of course you are then expected to be hospitable in return and somehow half the villagers will find their way by canoe to your boat to visit. It is quite fun having them come on board the boat and asking all sorts of question. This is when we wished we had plenty of pictures of home to show them, or perhaps a large picture book of San Francisco to share with them. It would have helped with the conversation since once you have discussed the boat, the village, the weather and the fishing we found we were at a loss. But they were very well mannered and delightful to have as visitors. The children in Fiji seemed especially well mannered. If you told them not to use the inflatable as a trampoline they would do as you asked.

Inflatable boats must be considered as disposable. We recently had to replace ours. One year in the tropical sun had destroyed the fabric. Unfortunately it was red, and red is a terrible color for the tropical sun. Even rigging line that is red deteriorates faster then any other color. Avon doesn't guarantee their red fabric, and they are one of the premiere manufacturers of dingys. Ours was a cheap copy, but the new one we purchased is a gray Avon, and hopefully it will hold up longer. The longer you are cruising the more you realize that there is no way of predicting in advance, sitting in a marina in S.F. Bay, what will be important to you, individually, in the way of equipment. Everyone we met had altered their opinions as they cruised. Things they felt were requirements at home soon faded and other things became absolutely necessary. For Mark and me having a large fast dingy has proved a major requirement. Mark is absolutely addicted to snorkeling and with two adults, and snorkeling equipment for both of us, we need a powerful engine to get the boat up on a plane and then we can go anywhere within a radius of several miles to snorkel, leaving Arietta in a safe anchorage. For others a little rowing bathtub would be perfectly adequate. There is no one and only way to cruise. Everyone approaches it from a different angle then after awhile, changes that angle to fit the reality of their own individual cruising experience. The one constant for Mark and me is joy in having a performance-oriented boat. We love to sail and this boat sails well. We seldom hand steer and with two people and days and days, or even weeks of 24 hours sailing that is a good thing. Between the Aries, a wind powered steering device, and the Auto helm, a battery powered steering device, we seldom ever need to hand steer. On a spinnaker reach though, Mark is still like a kid out of school playing racer and enjoying it to the max. In the Yasawa Islands for Fiji I probably did more snorkeling than anywhere else in our trip. There were so many places where the water was not too deep and the water was warm enough to spend hours and hours without ever getting too cold. For a diver it might not be a paradise, but for me it was perfect.

The trip from Fiji to N.Z. was definitely not a spinnaker run. It is approximately 1100 miles and we covered half the distance in three days. The wind was forward of the beam but not a hard beat, just a fast close reach. The wind went light and ahead in the last 200 miles so it took 8 days altogether. After so long in the tropics N.Z. was a sight for sore eyes. I think one would tire of anything if you experienced it for too long and we were definitely ready for a change of scenery. The smell of pine trees almost made my cry. It is strange sensation after so long in tropical waters having to rely on the chart and not being able to see the bottom, under the boat, in 30 or 40 feet of water.

New Zealand proved to be a work place for us. We hauled the boat and did the bottom and installed a new stove. The old one had come with the boat and finally rusted to the point of being dangerous. Flames would frequently shoot out the back when the oven was on. It ended up on the dumpster at the end of the Opua Wharf. The new stove is so much nicer with many more features, such as a broiler and it is stainless. It should last a very long time. The alternator had to be fixed and the poor old Volvo MD2B had gotten so tired it refused to start. Rings, valves, guy things, that will forever be a mystery to me, set it in fine shape and thanks to a fellow cruiser's careful instructions, Mark was able to do the work himself. Of course, it was a mess to live with. Imagine having a diesel engine torn apart in the middle of your living room, in a very tiny apartment, for two weeks.

We didn't travel around N.Z. as much as we would have liked to. The economy of the country is in dreadful state and we found it to be an expensive place to visit on our very conservative cruising budget. However, I did go to Auckland to visited with Terry Holliway, the woman who was my roommate the last time I cruised to N.Z. fifteen years ago. That time I ended up living in NZ for well over a year. It was one of those reunions where it seems as if the years totally fall away, and the conversation picks up as though you had seen each other only yesterday. It was a truly delightful visit, and a testimony to resilience of true friendship. On the bus to Auckland from Russell, as we came over the last hill, the beauty of Auckland Harbor and the Hairangi Gulf almost took my breath away. Seldom do you return to a place you loved, after many years, to find it to be even _more_ beautiful than you remembered. Usually you find your memory has enhanced the image, but not in this case. New Zealand is a treasure.

In the Bay of Islands we raced a few times in local club races. There was a woman's race I was asked to crew in and upon arriving discovered a man onboard. It seems the definition of woman's racing in the Opua Club is that a woman must be on the helm. I was reminded of "Powder Puff" races in SF Bay years ago where a "Bilge Rat" was allowed onboard. The husband of the woman who owned the boat wasn't along; he had sent his best friend to 'keep an eye on the little woman'. She had done very little racing, actually, but we managed to take first place beating boats that her husband had never beaten. It gave Carol such a dose of self-confidence she has since formed an all woman crew and is racing on a regular basis. Good for you! While we were in the Bay of Islands there was a great deal going on related to the 150th anniversary of the Treaty of Waitangi. Queen Elizabeth II and Prince Philip attended, and it was a tremendous undertaking with various activities over several weeks. One was a Tall Ship Regatta with seven huge square-riggers participating. The race consisted of two divisions. The first, the square-riggers, encouraged to use their engine at the start line, for the photographers benefit, and on the weather legs in order to finish this week, or even this century. The second division consisted of two-masted boats and we felt privileged to be invited to crew on an absolutely beautiful schooner. It was certainly a different sort of sailing than we were used to on our rather simply rigged sloop. We were introduced to weird things like golly wobblers and foretop sails. A slow race, but an excellent opportunity to take photos of the gorgeous square-riggers. Waitangi Day itself was sunny and warm and we totally enjoyed ourselves. An exciting air show by the N.Z. Air Force shook the air with the roar of their engines as they passed so close that your feared they might snag the top of the mast—very exhilarating. Entertainment was provided including one I particularly enjoyed—a concert of opera's favorite arias. Others preferred the folk singers and dancers and comedy companies, but there truly was something to please everyone. Amazingly, all of it was free to the public and consequently very well attended.

We had planned to cross the Tasman Sea in January but because of the diesel repairs, haul out and generally loving our time in NZ, it was March before we finally left. The Tasman has a bad reputation as a nasty bit of water. It is 1200 miles from Opua to Sydney so even though there is excellent weather forecasting available from the NZ weather department it is just too far to tell what might develop before you get all the way across. For three weeks prior to our leaving it had been perfect and for the first seven days we had the same incredibly beautiful sailing weather. Then it hit us. A cyclone formed in the Coral Sea, and a huge low developed off the New South Wales Coast. The cyclone named "Hilda" merged with the low to form what they kept referring to on the weather service report as a "complex low". We were in it. We hove to for two and a half days. Our wind speed indicator was pegged on 60 knots for the whole of one night and we had force 10 winds for most of the rest. I celebrated my birthday during this frightful storm and wondered if I would live to see another one. One wave broke over us and ripped out the dodger. We tried to use the storm tri sail (teensy weensy sail) but the U bolt on the baby stay deck traveler broke. Hove to, with no sails at all we were still heeled over 20 degrees. At one point, we tried to sail with just the storm jib but found we were blasting along at 8 knots, far too fast in those huge seas, an invitation for a disaster. When the wind finally moderated to 35 knots it seemed like a pleasant Sunday sail. During the time we were hove to we covered almost 100 miles passing directly over Taupo seamount, notorious for nasty seas at the best of times. All in all, it was one ocean sail I hope never to repeat although it was certainly an exciting experience—in retrospect. I'm sure it will give us a few good tales to tell at the Yacht Club Bar some day. What surprised me most was how calm I stayed. Both of us seemed afraid of upsetting the other so we spoke softly and calmly. Absolutely nothing you could do to change where you were, so just grit your teeth and do what you have to do. I guess in a real crisis I don't freak out or panic, which is a good thing to know about myself. Of course, the little daily annoyances are another thing entirely. In the end the amount of damage was not too bad, especially considering another boat in the same storm sent out a Mayday and barely made it to shore without sinking. With a torn mainsail, a torn jib, a bit of water in our instruments and the baby stay fitting as our total damage we feel fortunate, since it is all easily repairable—thank goodness. No structural hull damage or serious rigging failures. Love this boat!

We dried out, repaired and rested and think Sydney is a fabulous, beautiful city. After N.Z. it is inexpensive and there is so much fresh produce available it is a dream. A couple we met in French Polynesia lives here. They have been wonderful showing us around and helping find things. They recommended several cruising guides for our sail from Sydney to Darwin and we have found any cruising guides, even the worst are better than none. Right now we look forward to cruising the extensive bays and inlets of Pittwater and Broken Bay before heading up the coast.

Hope this finds everyone happy and healthy and in the mood to write letters. We do love to hear from home no matter what the length of the letter.

Best to everyone

Laraine

Letter 7
Australia

We certainly have covered a lot of distance, climate zones and culturally diverse areas since I last wrote. Our stay in Sydney seemed mostly a recovery from the Tasman crossing. Our friends, folks we met in French Polynesia who completed an eight year cruise, whisked us off to their home for real in-the-tub hot baths, beautifully prepared gourmet meals, video movies in front of the fireplace, and a lesson in hospitality we won't soon forget. They took us for a well-narrated tour of the Sydney, Blue Mountain and Pittwater areas, and to a wildlife reserve where I was able to pet a real live Koala bear. Besides being a wonderful host and hostess Michael and Norma Henderson helped find someone to repair our instruments and Norma, a former sail maker, did the repairs to the main and jib and put our dodger back together. Michael straightened out an error in our clearance into Australia. They had us down as 36 meters not 36 feet. He saved us $150 fee for vessels over 50 feet and helped us fill in our request for a cruising permit (you must list every place that you plan to stop in Australia). He also told us about the two cruising guides written by Alan Lucas, one for New South Wales, the other for Queensland, without which we would probably have had innumerable problems. So, it was a very sad day when we left such dear friends behind in Sydney.

I guess the biggest question in cruising Australia East Coast is "Are we out of our Mind?" Actually that's not quite that bad, but it is certainly a major challenge, and once there, you have no other choice but to continue! Outside of the Sydney, Pittwater, and Broken Bay areas, which really are delightful cruising ground, there are very, few places to anchor, other than open roadsteads. Otherwise, you must cross bars and boy can that be tricky. If must be timed well with the rising and falling tides and can be treacherous if a large swell is running. I know now why multi hulls and shoal draft boats are so popular here. Our seven-foot draft was the absolute maximum in most places and a few places we dared not risk at all. Crossing some of those bars gave me an understanding of the term surfing. In spite of having to cross the bar at the entrance, the Camden Haven/ Laurieton area was undoubtedly worth any amount of trouble to get there! It is a delightful small town, friendly and relaxed, pretty enough to please any photographer. A mountain acts as a scenic background for the town. Besides being a lovely setting it affords a magnificent view of the coast, both north and south as far as you can see. Of course you need to have the energy to make the two-hour hike to the top. By slow dingy, the trip up river to the town of Kendal, on glassy smooth water, bounded by willow-lined banks with pastures beyond, was, without doubt, the most peaceful afternoon we spent in Australia.

The contrast to this area and the Gold Coast area of Queensland, with its huge hotels, casinos, frantic shopping complexes, and nightclubs was a tremendous culture shock. The latter, not really our cup of tea, was interesting to observe. The big boom in tourism in Australia has resulted in a glut of tourist-oriented business throughout Queensland. More a place for young hip kids than middle age cruisers on a tight budget.

One of the things we naively looked forward to in Australia was cruising the Great Barrier Reef. Well, it was a bit of a disappointment. Yes, there are hundred of miles of reef and coral islands, but due to the unusual and heavy rain this year the water was very murky. The lack of clarity of the water and all the reef and bars and islands produces a bit of a navigational challenge. We were told, if you get out to the very outer edges of the reef you have clear water but unfortunately that isn't where you go in a sailboat. It is a long way with no decent anchorage. Perhaps on a perfectly calm day with no wind at all, you could motor out, drop an anchor on the edge of the reef and hope the conditions didn't change in the middle of the night. The alternative is to go to a tourist center and take an excursion on one of the fast charter catamarans that take divers out. The next time I come here I will have a budget to enable me to take advantage of all that the barrier reef has to offer, but this time I am afraid we will miss a lot. It is said to be spectacular in the right places. We did do some snorkeling, but it was not what we had anticipated.

The weather along the Queensland coast is highly unpredictable, or it certainly was when we were there. Luckily, we were safely anchored in Airley Beach when a huge low developed, unexpectedly, and resulted in the loss of one boat and a crew of four. Another boat was lost but the crew, fortunately rescued and several boats limped into port with considerable damage. Another low developed as we were sailing from one island to another but we made it to the anchorage (although we had only about ½ mile visibility in pelting rain) before the worst of it hit. One boat went on a reef that night. The crew of eight managed to cling to the reef until rescued, but the boat was demolished.

The Australian Weather Bureau mentioned neither of these storms until at least two days after they hit. After the impressively efficient weather reporting, and sea watch, in New Zealand, we thought the Australians a bit lax.

With the weather, the reefs, the huge currents (tidal differences of up to 20 feet) this is not an easy area to cruise. Also the trade winds are strong so the swells make crossing the bars challenging. It is definitely not relaxed laid back cruising. You need to be taking bearings the whole time and we avoided anything but day sailing since sailing at night was far too stressful and totally sleepless.

The farther north you go (as the weather starts to get warmer) there are fewer places where you can safely swim. Until I saw the movie, "Crocodile Dundee" I had no idea that Australia had crocks, but wow—do they ever. In the Escape River we spotted a couple of the beauties sunning themselves on shore. They must have been 12 or 14 feet long and the next day there was dear old grand-daddy about 18 feet long. Really scary!

We finally rounded "The Top"—Cape York. The distance from Sydney to the top of Queensland is just about the same as Portland Oregon to Cabo San Lucas, Mexico. A long way to sail.

At one point in our trip north from Sydney we debated continuing north to New Guinea and then possibly keep going that way and head back to California by way of the North Pacific—a vague plan, but not impossible to work out if we decided to go that way. However, we are now committed to continuing west. That means we have basically decided to continue on around the world! A big decision, because we are far from half way yet but close to the point of no return from a practical sailing point of view. A circumnavigation is a dream I have had for a long time, and happily Mark has decided to make it his goal as well. Once past Cape York it felt like we were in the tropics again, sailing at night in shorts. Wonderful!

Each year the Darwin Yacht Club sponsors a "Race" from Darwin to Ambon, Indonesia. The entrants this year, 60 in number, consist of perhaps 10 actual racing yachts and 50 cruisers. This may sound odd but the red tape involved in getting a cruising permit for Indonesia is such that entering the race, paying the entry fee, and letting them handle the paper work, ends up being the easiest, and in some cases the most economical way to go. Besides, it is fun. You are required to have a safety inspection which forced us to have our life raft serviced and our flares updated and you must hand steer which means they require three adults on each vessel. We feel fortunate we had an Ausie, Andrew McCullough, as our crew. He was competent, cheerful, not a picky eater (since we had to hand steer

24 hrs a day I had limited time to cook) and we.both enjoyed his pleasant, easy going company.

The race left Darwin July 28 and we arrived in Ambon Aug 1. There are three divisions, Multi Hull, Racing and Cruising. If it were up to the entrants the Racing division would consist of 3 or 4 boats so the race committee made the decision as to who is a racer and who is a cruiser and it doesn't have anything to do with the fact that you are actually cruisers. Anyway, they put us in the racing division and of course the serious racers were the winners, but we had a good time and the festivities in Ambon were great. Parties and dinners and so many new people to meet and enjoy. What a great way to start our visit to this fascinating, diverse, amazing country of Indonesia. One of my larger challenges in Indonesia was going into town by myself and through hand signals, and an occasional person who understood tiny bit of English, managed to get a stamp made for our boat. Stamping documents in this part of the world somehow makes them more official. Getting a custom made stamp and an inked stamp pad took me all day, but when I got back to the yacht harbor there were a few people who were surprised that I managed to do it alone. I was actually quite proud of myself. Something that would be so simple at home seemed almost an insurmountable task in a place where you cannot speak the language. Of course, it would have been impossible to learn the language of every country we visited, no matter how advantageous that would have been.

Continued. Indonesia

I must admit, until very recently, my knowledge of the geographic location of the countries of South East Asia was abysmally lacking. I certainly could not visualize, in my mind, the location of the various countries and really had no idea of the number of islands that make up the country of Indonesia. I had little idea of its people and their culture. I was actually quite apprehensive, as one hears stories of pirates and theft and heavy-handed officials looking for bribes, but I must say that we personally, had absolutely no bad experiences at all in the time we were in Indonesian waters. It is a wonderful place to visit.

Ambon, our first stop is located in the Maluccas Group known to early explorers as the fabled "Spice Islands". After spending time in sparsely populated Pacific Islands one does experience a bit of a people shock here. Indonesia is the fifth most populace country in the world and the areas that are fertile are densely populated, Ambon especially.

Most tourists to Indonesia visit Bali, or Java, where the capital Djakarta is located. A few resorts have been built on Lompoc Island, across from Bali, but it takes a particularly intrepid, adventurer, usually a determined backpacker, to travel very far beyond those easily accessible areas. That is one of the beauties of traveling by yacht. You can get to places the average traveler never has the opportunity to visit. Of course some places really have very little to see or do from the point of view of someone with a 2 week vacation and Ambon is one of these, but for those of us cruising the area it was fascinating. There is air service between Darwin and Ambon but not really any great tourist attractions. The result is that anyone who is fair skinned, fair-haired, with anything other than brown eyes, really stands out in a crowd. It is quite an odd feeling to have everyone on a crowded street staring at you. Some want to touch you and everyone says, "Hello Meester" or "Hello Meeses" and "Where do you come from"? English is a required subject in Indonesian schools but it is very basic. I think for most, lessons end after the above phrases. However, it seemed that anytime you venture into town someone, who really did want to learn English, would attach themselves to you and follow you around all day trying to improve their linguistic skills. At times, this was actually very useful, especially when trying to work out the prices for items in the huge outdoor markets in Ambon. You can easily learn to say, "How much does it cost"? But then you need to understand the answer, a bit of a problem since some things are per item and other per kilo and I never could remember how to count from 1 to 10.

The festivities for the race lasted about one week and after that yachts gradually left Ambon. There is so much of Indonesia to see, and our visa only allowed us two months in the country. We knew we would have to miss many places and touch far to lightly on others, but we decided to cover as much as we could in the time allowed. The people of Indonesia are very diverse in their cultures and religions. A huge Muslim country, but with large areas that are still Christian as result of the Portuguese and Dutch colonials. The Islands of Flories and Timor are predominately Christian. Bali is totally different from anywhere else in Indonesia. It is almost all Indonesian Hindu and the beauty of its architecture; the abundance of skilled artisans, as well as the famous Balinese dances, reflects this influence.

From Ambon we sailed to Buton Straights between Butung Island and Suluwesi (Celebes). The children here were very aggressive, swarming around the boat in their little dugout canoes demanding candy and pencils and books and T-shirts. It got to the point that you would stay inside the boat rather than sit in the cockpit, since we quickly ran out of all the pencils and paper, and felt very mean not being able to give them something. They had so little and we wanted to be able to give them something. Even a simple pencil, nothing to us, was so appreciated. If you plan to visit this area I would advise you to have plenty of school supplies, since they are scarce.

Indonesia, being a nation of islands relies heavily on the sea for its food. Unfortunately, there is no control and conservation is an unknown word. In the Tiger Islands we saw huge flotillas of fishing boats, fishing at night with lanterns and the glow on the horizon resembled that of a large city. Hundred and hundreds of 20 to 30 foot catamarans with little houses built on them with racks for drying their catch. With no refrigeration all the fish are gutted, split and dried for transported to market. Anchoring down wind from a fishing fleet is not considered a prime anchorage. The lives of whole villages depends on fish. One shudders at the thought of what will happen when there are no more. Snorkeling on the reefs you seldom saw fish more than a couple of inches long.

The people in the Tiger Islands were, materially, the poorest people I've ever encountered. We went ashore to visit and they were very hospitable, certainly not demanding, but when they saw me disposing of usable containers, old vinegar bottles, and mayonnaise jars, even empty beer cans they asked for them. I felt guilty and somehow wasteful. Even our trash seemed a treasure to them. At one village the mayor invited us ashore and we had tea in his home. He was a Muslim with three wives, but said the government was trying to discourage the younger people from having more than one wife. Seeing the number of children in each village it seemed an excellent idea. There just aren't enough fish left.

The distance from Ambon to Flories 400–500 miles (as the crow does it) moves you from lush tropical productive land to dry brown desert-like landscape. The people here are very pleasant, friendly and curious but not at all aggressive. Next time, should be ever cruise this area again (somewhat unlikely, I'm afraid) we would spend more time in Flories and less in Buton, and the Tiger Islands.

The next absolutely required stop, although not really a great anchorage, is Komodo Island, home of the famous Komodo Dragons. Although there are dragons in other areas it is Komodo where they are kept in a fenced area readily available for viewing. The Dragons are really lizards, up to 13 feet long weighing up to 350 lbs. And they do not breathe fire. They are actually rather ugly and have been known to occasionally eat people. Usually, though they eat goats and small deer. There is a scheduled feeding time when you can go and view them tearing up and eating a baby goat, but I didn't think I could stand to see a cute little goat eaten in such a brutal manner so we avoided feeding time.

Bali, as I said before, is unique in Indonesia. Everything in the life of the Balinese revolves around their Hindu beliefs. It is a form of Hinduism that has evolved over the years in Bali and Java Islands. Their temples are beautiful, their buildings are works of art, and even the markers on the road indicating the end of one town and the beginnings of the next are artistic creations. The climate in Bali is wet, and the land fertile. The major crop is rice and their beautifully terraced, well-tended rice fields produce three crops per year. Bali is the area of Indonesia most tourist visit. It is a fun place, with Kutu Beach a great place to buy cheap clothes and souvenirs. If you really want quality items, you need to search a little harder, but they are certainly there.

The Balinese people are very creative and do beautiful carvings, both wood and stone and make jewelry and paintings and create marvelous tapestry fabrics. Even the fishing boats in the waters surrounding Bali were painted and were meant to be pretty as well as functional. Their brightly colored outriggers and bows with dragon mouths and eyes were lovely examples of their artistry. Unfortunately, in Bali, as elsewhere in Indonesia, there are too many fisherman and too few fish.

Our two-month visa expired too quickly, so we officially checked out of Indonesia bound for Singapore. We did take our time, however, anchoring overnight in several different spots along the way. In the areas between Kalimantan (Borneo) and Sumatra the fishing methods changed considerably. At first we were astonished by the huge fleets of little sailing boats we had to navigate and dodge at night. As we approached they would light a lamp and one by one hundreds of tiny lamps would appear. It seemed it would be impossible to thread our way through, but as we approached they would glide silently away leaving a path for us to follow. As we moved closer to Sumatra it changed and instead of the sail powered fishing boats we had seen thus far, we now began seeing little "houses" on stilts. They were scattered all over the place, some in rather deeper water than we would have thought possible. These huts had nets draped under them and, abandoned by day, were well lit up at night with fisherman coming at dusk and going back home at daybreak. We also encountered, motorized fishing boats of every description, some very prettily painted, others definitely working boats but most seemed to be powered with one cylinder diesels, looking well past their prime, and very noisy. They also fished at night and were frequently unlit. Here again, we had no problems since we kept our running lights on and they just stayed out of our way. They seemed to be quite used to dodging larger vessels. Although it made us nervous we never did hit any of them. A credit to their skills more than ours, since more often than not we couldn't see them as more than a dark though rather noisy shadow.

From a "third world" country such as Indonesia to the huge, ultra modern city of Singapore feels like a shift in a time warp. To anchor one night by a tiny village of thatch roofed houses populated by subsistence level fishing folk and the next day be riding one of the cleanest most efficient Mass Rapid Transit Systems in the world almost makes you dizzy. But, here we are. Singapore, 2.6 million people living in the world's smallest country—616 square kilometers (240.6 square miles). The world's busiest port, 2nd largest container port, third largest oil refining port and I think definitely the worlds' cleanest city. There are sign everywhere to wash your hands and huge fines for spitting—certainly different!

Will tell you all about it next time.

Goodbye for now, Laraine

Letter 8
Singapore & Malaysia & Thailand

Three weeks in Singapore was about enough time to spend. The novelty of a big, clean, efficient, impersonal city lasted a while, but the trip from the yacht anchorage into the city center was an hour there and an hour back. It made it an all day outing to go into town to get supplies and stock up for the next phase of our trip. It was a calm well-protected anchorage though, so we were not concerned about leaving the boat for long days away. The Changi Yacht Club located near, and named for, the infamous Japanese POW camp of WWII was lovely and we ate a few meals and did some socializing, but, as everything else in Singapore, a bit expensive for our tight budget. Still, Singapore is a great place to restock with western food and purchase necessary boat bits. It is not a good place to haul out though, as some of our friends found out. The fees were based on commercial vessels and they did not cater to small yachts.

This is probably the hottest place I have ever spent time in my life. The heat and humidity are suffocating. Sleeping naked in the cockpit one could scarcely breath and no number of cool showers in a day could stop you from feeling sticky and sweaty all the time. The harbor was far too dirty for swimming and, due to the huge oil facilities nearby, the air in the yacht anchorage always smelled like a refinery. The good thing about the long ride into town was that the rapid transit system was blissfully cool with air conditioning and I was temped to get on and not get off until it was time to leave Singapore. Luckily the Yacht Club had excellent amenities, wonderful showers, good food and icy cold beer. Still, it is an interesting city, but would be far more enjoyable, for me at lease, staying in an air-conditioned hotel in the heart of town. Maybe someday.

The next leg of the trip, up the coast of Malaysia, once had a reputation for being pirate waters. It is now a subject for yacht gossip, but in reality, small yachts are not bothered and any piracy that exists these days is big time theft from container ships. The bigger, less romantic, but far more present danger to a sailboat are the tremendous thunder squalls that come blasting across the Malacca Straights from Sumatra to the Malay Peninsula. Winds we experienced could go from 10 knots to 40, gusting to 55 in a matter of minutes and would last up to two hours. The lightening displays were breathtakingly beautiful, with up to 20 or 30 flashes per second. If it had not been for potential damage we would have thoroughly enjoyed the show but we personally knew five yachts with lightening damage. Two of them had all their electronics, satnav, radar, and SSB radio, even alternators on the engine totally blasted. Another had their VHF antenna reduced to a 2 inch black stump and an aluminum French yacht had the paint blister and peel from one side of the hull. Awesome!

Malaysia was a delightful surprise. It is a pleasant, relaxed, hassle free place to visit. English is widely spoken, since it is a former British colony. The West Coast has a strong Chinese influence and the Island city of Penang is mostly Chinese. The East Coast however is predominately Malay. It seems a thriving, affluent country and the people were polite, friendly, and well dressed. It is a place I could easily have spent more time. Maybe next time.

The down side of the picture is that the West Coast of Malaysia has several large rivers dumping quantities of silt into the ocean. This creates, large mud flats and water that has little clarity. In addition there are huge schools of jellyfish making swimming unappealing and while they are not deadly they inflict a painful sting. This tends to reduce the temptation to jump into the water to cool off, even though it was devilish hot. The symbol on the Yacht Club burgee for the Lamut Y.C. is a jellyfish. It was the cutest Yacht Club—if that adjective should be applied to a Yacht Club. It had a sort of thatched hut building and they served wonderful huge plates of prawns, and ice-cold beer, well within our budget. What a pleasant place to while away a hot afternoon with friends.

The Island of Lankawai is the last stop in Malaysia and a duty free port. This is the place to stock up on beer. Just about every brand known to man is available and they do a roaring business. There are innumerable lists of other items available as well, but ghetto blasters, bone china, and crystal aren't hot items on a small sailboat.

Next stop, Thailand. Couldn't wait to eat out a lot. It seems every country is a surprise in some way but what amazed me about Thailand were the number of tourists, especially Germans. I guess northern Europe in December is a bit cold and the travel brochures for Phi Phi and Phuket look ever so inviting with their aqua water and sandy beaches. But, viewing the beaches one wonders if anyone is left in Germany? I have never been anywhere that seemed so overrun, almost, but not quite, to the point of being ruined, by tourists. On the other hand, it was a totally fun place to visit. The water, although an improvement over Malaysia is still far from crystal clear and there is very little coral. I fear the reefs in the Tuamotes, Tonga and Fiji have spoiled us. At least here there were no jellyfish so it was great to be able to cool off. The best thing about Thailand, if you like spicy, is the food. It was cheap and wonderful and we ate out almost every night. All the way up the Malaysian coast we took great care not to sunburn our lips in anticipation of the spicy cuisine, and it was worth it. Thailand is a fascinating county, but unfortunately we didn't have the budges to allow us to travel inland, although I would have loved to visit Bangkok. Friends who did considerable traveling told us that all the way up on the Thailand, Burma, Laos border, as far from the beaten path as they ever thought to go, their driver pointed out an area being developed into a world class golf course, resort and modern gambling casino, by the Japanese.

We spent Christmas on the beach in Nai Harn Bay, Phuket, under beach umbrellas, with folks from 8 or 10 other yachts. Andrew, our Aussie crew from Darwin to Ambon Race had sailed on two other yachts from Ambon to Bali, then Bali to Singapore and showed up in Phuket to spend Christmas and New Years with "his cruising family". It was a lazy congenial day, perhaps not unusual to the "Down Under" crowd but a change from "traditional Christmas" for this former Canadian.

On New Years Eve, Phatong, the largest tourist center in Thailand, becomes one huge party. The number of bars is staggering and it is quite a surprise after spending time in several subdued Muslim countries like Malaysia, and most of Indonesia. Thailand must be one of the most "free" places there is. Prostitution is blatant and VD clinics are common sites on almost every corner. It is actually a bit frightening, especially when we saw so many young service men on their way to the Gulf wandering around with young ladies on their arm. I kept thinking "I'm glad I'm not their mother." New years Eve Phatong style was a hoot. We ate with friends then spent the evening with other boating buddies at a bar favored by the yachting crowd. Fireworks went off all night and the streets were full of party goes since almost all of the bars are open air. You can simply wander from one to the next with a drink in your hand getting a refill wherever you are. One bar might have better music and one serves better drinks, or colder beer or better snacks. So the whole town becomes one big party. What a wild and crazy night, but it was a great, fun, New Years Eve. I was surprised, next day, when I went ashore early to pick up fresh veggies for our New Years Day brunch, to see people still going strong in the bars at 8:00am. They certainly do party heartily around here. The red paper from the firecrackers was ankle deep and the whole town center still smelled of black powder, curry, whiskey and beer.

After departing Thailand most of our friends headed to Sri Lanka but Mark and I had had enough of heavily populated, hectic places, with too much red tape. Mark loves swimming and exploring isolated islands so instead of Sri Lanka we took off for the Chagos Archipelago. This is all that is left of B.I.O.T. (British Indian Ocean Territory) and it is leased to the American Military. It consists of Solomon Atoll, Peros Banjos Atoll, the Great Chagos Bank and the American base of Diego Garcia. With the exception of Diego Garcia Military base, which is off limits, yachts are free to visit the other areas and can come and go as they please. The British administer the area and fly over to check on it. They also occasionally come up to visit, in person, by ship, bringing a few fresh supplies. Since we were there during the Kuwait War, however, they were much too busy to be sociable.

There are no residents left in Chagos, since that was one of the conditions of the Americans leasing the area. All the inhabitants were moved to other islands in the Indian Ocean, particularly the Seychelles. There is no access, except by private vessel. A few of the islands have ruins of building and a few remaining breadfruit and lime trees, a remnant of British Colonial days, but otherwise it is empty. We have been here a month and in that time seen and spoken to only seven other yachts. Two planes circled low to check out the visitors and, other than B52s flying back and forth from Diego Garcia to the Gulf War, we have had complete peace and solitude. It seems so strange to be in this peaceful paradise and see warplanes flying overhead. The War in Kuwait began when we were about half way between Thailand and Chagos and who knows when it will end.

We still talk on the radio to friends in Sri Lanka and India and will join up with them again, but listening to their description of dirty harbors and official hassles, especially in India, we are glad we sailed the extra miles to get here. It was one of the best passages ever. We covered the 1800 miles in 12 ½ extremely pleasant days of wonderful sailing.

It may seem odd to someone viewing the map of the Indian Ocean, that we sailed all the distance from Thailand to Chagos simply to visit an atoll. Why not some other islands? Unfortunately governments of the islands in the Indian Ocean are not very hospitable. The Nicobars, Andamans and Lakshadweep Islands simply do not allow visiting yachts. A very limited number of tourists are permitted, but they are restricted to specific resort areas. The inhabitants are Islamic and do no want their culture influenced by outsiders. Having seen how some of the tourists behaved in Thailand I don't blame them.

The officials in some islands allow you to stay two weeks then start charging heavy fees to encourage you to leave and you are only allowed to anchor in approved area. The Seychelles charge from day one and make the paper work such a hassle that few yachts stay long. Unfortunately, that doesn't leave much cruising in the Indian Ocean, although recently Madagascar and Mozambique have opened up, so for those intending to round South Africa it offers a new perspective.

I will end this letter now and hope everyone had a good Christmas and a Happy New Year.

Bye for now, Laraine

Letter 9
Yemen & the Red Sea

After one month we decided we could no longer rationalize staying in Chagos. We sincerely regretted leaving but, with no fresh produce available, and the prospect of headwinds for the full length of the Red Sea, if we delayed too long, we reluctantly departed.

When we left Chagos on February 20th, the Kuwait War was still a considerable concern. The ground war had not begun and no one realized the end would come so soon. We tentatively headed for Djibouti in the Gulf of Aden but if the war escalated or any terrorist activity threatened the Suez Canal we could divert to Kenya. Of course the end of the war came quickly and instead of Djibouti we sailed for Aden, which is a much less expensive and easier place to prepare for the Red Sea.

From Chagos to Aden is about 2500 miles. We experienced very light winds for the first several days from due north, but happily the wind picked up and the direction changed and we covered the distance in 20 days.

In mid 1990 the Peoples Democratic Republic of Yemen, a Marxist regime merged with the Yemen Arab Republic and threw out the Russians. The new unified country of Yemen is pleased with their status and pleased that their hostilities have ceased and anyone you talk to happily tells you so. The result of this unification for someone visiting the port of Aden is that you can travel inland into some of the most fascinating country I've ever seen. Relatively un-traveled by tourists it offered us a unique experience. With 5 yachtie friends, we rented a mini Toyota van, to explore inland. We drove through ancient country, where the mountains seem to go straight up but somehow manage to support a town on the very top of each peak. I'm sure they were built this way so they could be easily defended. The hillsides are terraced and one wonders how long it must take to travel from the mountain tops to the fields hundreds of feel below, and how the women must struggle hauling water all the way up those hills.

The capital city of Yemen is Sana. Legend tells us that it was Noah's son who founded the city after the flood and in truth there has been a city located there since pre-history. The present city is rather unique. The architectural style goes back to about 100 years BC and the current buildings themselves are several hundred years old. There are many windows with alabaster windowpanes, even today.

Unfortunately, even here the Japanese auto industry has done wonders polluting the air. I'm sure the emission standards are not up to the State of California. There were no European or American vehicles. However, if you turn into an alley, too narrow for cars, it is easy to believe you have stepped back several hundred years into a world of women veiled from heat to toe in black and men in long robes armed with curved daggers bringing back memories of tales from the Arabian Nights.

Being fair haired and unveiled it was hard to keep a low profile although we tried, since Yemen had sided with Iraq in the Gulf War, just weeks ago. We didn't go around waving the Stars and Stripes and were a wee bit nervous at first. Although people stared at us as though we were creatures from another planet we experienced no hostilities. On the contrary, almost everyone was hospitable and friendly. Of course, if anyone asked where we were from we said New Zealand (one of our group was from there). Most of the Yemenis had never heard of it—which damaged our Kiwi friend's ego, but protected us from any anti American sentiments.

Seeing women veiled in black from head to toe, faces covered, was odd at first. Our guide said that it was only in public, since it is considered impolite for women to expose themselves, but at home they wore colorful clothing and judging by the vividly colored clothing for sale in the shops, I guess they do.

It was the first place we had been where the local men did not wear jeans and T-shirts at least some of the time. It was the most foreign, exotic-feeling place I've ever experience and absolutely fascinating.

Aden, the port for Yemen, has the easiest check in procedures we had encountered anywhere. Travelling by yacht the paper work can drive you crazy. It can sometimes take a full day to clear in, customs, health, port authorities, immigration, and then when you leave another full day to clear out. If all you want to do is top up with diesel and water and purchase a few tomatoes, this can drive you mad. Aden was a pleasure.

Somewhere between Chagos and Aden we passed the ½ way mark. Half the way around the world from where we began. The part of the whole trip around the world I dreaded most was, however, directly ahead—the Red Sea. This particular piece of water has a dreadful reputation, which it has worked hard to earn and certainly deserves. It is a totally schizophrenic place; nice one moment and a monster the next, but to get from the Indian Ocean to the Med, there is no practical alternative.

Generally, the winds in the Red Sea blow from the north, which is wonderful if you want to go from the Med south, but for those heading north it means 1200 miles of beating into headwinds. If you are very lucky during the first three months of the year, you might possibly get winds from the south for about 1/3 of the distance, but beyond that, headwinds. So, leaving Aden with southerly winds we just hoped they would follow us up, through the Straits of Bab al Man dab (Arabic for Gates of Hell) into the Red Sea.

We passed through Bab al Man dab at sunrise with 20–25 knots southerly winds. As we moved through into open water we expected the wind to fan out and decrease. So much for that theory. As the day progressed the wind increased. We did want a tail wind, but this was ridiculous. We had strong gale force winds by lunchtime and the first anchorage was 75 miles from Bab-al-Man dab. The seas increased in size rapidly, but it was their steepness and how close together they were to each other that made them intimidating. We arrived at the anchorage well before dark and sat out the worst of the winds in company with 7 other yachts we knew well.

The wind decreased to a more sensible 25–30 knots and we set off again to try to put some miles behind us. The tailwinds held for two more days, then, within a few hours it changed to gale force winds from the north-northwest. Once again it was the short steep seas that were the problem. Luckily, the gale force winds only lasted about six hours and gradually moderated so we could make good time again, although beating into uncomfortable seas. At the next anchorage we had to put away the spinnaker, the 150, 130, 100, 90 and the storm jibs. That tells the story of the day's winds.

The first third of the Red Sea borders on Ethiopia on the west, and Saudi Arabia on the east. Ethiopia has been in the grip of civil unrest for a long time. Gunboats patrol the coast, probably to discourage arms smuggling, but they occasionally fire on yachts, so it is best to stay clear of that shore. Saudi Arabia simply discourages visitors for religious reasons, so if you need to anchor, as we did, you just hope to find an uninhabited island, not too close to an unfriendly coast.

Once north of Ethiopia, Sudan is more hospitable but even there it is best to get north of Port Sudan before stopping on the mainland since they also have a rebellion going on.

Between Bab-al-Man dab and Port Sudan we experienced two gales and anchored three nights on the most desolate, uninhabitable, bleak islands imaginable, but at least they offered sufficient shelter to allow a good night sleep.

The Sudan Coast form Port Sudan north can be quite pleasant, as it is possible to day sail from anchorage to anchorage. We did this for a while. Beating into 20 knots is OK for a day if you follow it with a good night sleep in a calm spot. However, when the wind turned southerly we took advantage of it and covered a good distance before the next northerly hit. This one wasn't too bad so we day sailed again. The farther north the more severe the northerlies become. We spent 6 days in one anchorage with the wind reading 35-to 45 the whole time. It finally moderated and again we made a dash north. This time the anchorage was a bit farther and we were 20 miles from it when we got hit again with wind gusting 35–45. We finally make it in and sat out the rest of the night in a rather bouncy anchorage.

We did, finally, make Port Suez. Our conclusion on Red Sea sailing is that you have to have a boat that sails very well to windward or you need a big engine, a big prop, and lots of fuel. Our tiny 2 blade-folding prop means we sail and luckily Arietta is a great weatherly vessel. I felt sorry for friends with boats that don't go well to weather and don't really power well either. It makes it slow, and dreadfully hard to claw your way upwind.

Although the Red Sea hadn't been the horror my wild imagination had pictured I was glad to see it end. The dust and salt take days to wash off. Sails, halyards and rigging have to be scrubbed thoroughly. Even inside, the boat was full of salt and dust. With no water maker, no rain and no idea how long you have to sit out the numerous storms, you certainly can't waste drinking water washing the boat. Now we are in Suez there is ample water readily available so we are doing a massive housecleaning.

We hadn't fueled up since Aden and used just four jerry jugs all the way to Suez, including charging batteries as well as motoring. I almost wish we were in need of fuel since this seems to be the cheapest place in the world to by diesel. Five cents a liter and an additional five cents if they deliver directly to the boat. Amazing. Our trip up the Red Sea is over. We had no damage at all and actually had some good sailing, so no complaints.

The red tape and paperwork in Egypt become so overwhelming that you simply hire an agent. If you get a good one, it is well worth it. Ours called himself "The Prince of the Red Sea". He proved to be very professional, honest and knowledgeable.

We could not come to Egypt without seeing the pyramids and Cairo so we got together with the same travelling friends from Yemen, and made a day trip to the big city and all its museums and antiquities. I got to ride a camel around the Sphinx! If only Mommy could see me now! The Egyptian museum is quite overwhelming. A few hours cannot do it justice. The highlight is the King Tut exhibit, which we had seen a few years ago in San Francisco when it was on tour. It is just as impressive the second time around.

We found the average Egyptian to be friendly and polite. In the shop the ladies shoved me to the head of the line to get bread or meat and everyone thought America and George Bush were "Number One." The officials however are totally corrupt. Having an agent insulates you somewhat, but you still have to deal with the Suez Canal pilots and the officials in Port Said who all want "presents" or a bribe. Baksheesh it is called, and they accept it as being totally normal. In fact if someone does not take advantage a position like that their countrymen consider them a fool. You just have to keep cool and relax, and not let it bother you, but a Christian, Western work ethic makes this hard to accept.

We had a great sail from Egypt to Cyprus. Although the predicted weather report kept us very nervous, we actually made good time. The winds were on the beam, first from the east, then after some quick shifting of spinnaker gear (raise the pole, jibe the pole, lower the pole) from the west.

Cyprus is wonderful. The red tape is minimal, the officials are polite and honest, it's clean, friendly and the food is great. I've seen food in the supermarkets I haven't seen since San Francisco. They are having a serious drought which means you cannot hose down the boat, but I can have a fresh water shower every single day—Wow! Amazing the simple things that please a cruiser. I even found a beauty salon and had a manicure and a haircut. Totally decadent!

So, now what? Some people cruise the Med for years and years. There are so many countries, islands, cultures and also a lot of yachts. We may get tired of crowded anchorages; we may like it, but at the moment don't have a clue what we will do. Will write again in a few months. Hope everyone is well. Would love to hear from you.

Bye for now

Laraine

Letter 10
the Med

It's amazing how few things in this cruising life ever turn out the way you anticipate. Places you expect to be romantic disappoint and places you never gave a second thought are the fascinating sites you will always remember. We spent three
weeks in Cyprus having a good time with friends we had met as far back as Mexico, and saying goodbye to too many of them. Once you reach the Med the
camaraderie, which has been so wonderful through the hardship and uncertainty
of the third world, dissolves. Not because anyone wants it to, but because the des-
tinations are so varied and the schedules so diverse. A few folks put their boats up
in Cyprus and return home to take care of business immediately, with the plan of
returning to the cruising life in a year or two. Others have unlimited time to
spend cruising the Med and visiting Europe, while still others plan to spend one
season only and then cross the Atlantic for homes on the East coast. Still other,
like us, head for the Caribbean and the Panama Canal before returning to the
West Coast. Of course, for our European cruising friends, their journey is almost
over. Our plans, as usual, were as solid as quicksand. We thought we might spend
the season cruising the Eastern Med then return to Cypress, put the boat up and
work for a while, then cruise the Western Med the following year. Unfortunately,
the more we thought about it the less practical it seemed, but when we left
Cypress we made a reservation to haul out in the fall to keep our options open.

Cypress is a divided island. Turkey occupies the northern third of the island,
and the capital, Nicosia, is a divided city, patrolled by United Nations troops. If
you wish to visit Greece you cannot go to the occupied portion of Cypress and if
you ever plan to return to the southern part of Cypress you cannot enter the
occupied portion. The Turks, however, place no restrictions on anyone visiting
Cypress. We left Larnaca for Turkey, having checked the weather report, but
within four hours were into nasty seas and 35 knot headwinds. The updated
weather report predicted gale force winds on the south coast of Cyprus. We
decided the sensible thing to do was return to Larnaca, although Mark did so
reluctantly, hating to give up. I had no such reluctance and happily returned.

We had the distinction of being the last of the boats that left that day to turn around. Two days later we set off again. We sailed about 1/3 of the way in very light winds and finally had to motor most of the remaining distance. Even our lightest sails hung limp and the sea surface resembled a reflecting pond. This pattern of gales and calms is the sort of weather that followed us throughout our entire stay in the Med. It is the reason most people we met told us that Mediterranean sailing was not exactly great. Although I enjoyed seeing places we visited I cannot recommend the Med as a good place to sail just for fun.

In our travels we became good friends with a couple who were just completing a circumnavigation with the homeport of Salonica, Greece. They had spent years cruising the Greek islands prior to their big trip around the world and Mark spent several days discussing Greek Island sailing with them. We were so glad later that he had. The recommended tactic was to day sail near the coast of Turkey as far as north as we wanted to go, and then head west or south, but definitely not try to sail northeast in the islands in the summer, especially in the Cycladies. Keeping this in mind we checked into Turkey at Finike. I'm glad we began our visit to Turkey in this particular spot because it gave us such a good first impression, which would not have been the case, I'm afraid, had we entered at a more heavily tourist town. Finike is slightly off the beaten track as there isn't much to attract tourists in the way of beaches or ruins. We liked it for its lack of tourist attractions and the friendly attitude of the town's people. English is taught in the schools, so most of the young people, at least, have a smattering of English and one has no trouble getting along. Thanks to the amazing foresight of Kemel Ataturk, the dynamic leader of Turkey from the early 1920's to the late 1930's Turkey is far more European than its Muslim neighbors. He outlawed the wearing of the fez, the symbol of the decadent Ottoman Empire. He gave the vote to women and got rid of their traditional veiled, head to toe, garb. He also brought in the use of the Roman alphabet to replace the Arabic script, hoping to direct the destiny of Turkey towards the west, not east. If the Cypress problem can ever be resolved Turkey may see Ataturk's dreams realized. His statue is seen in every park and square, and even the young people I spoke to consider him to be a hero.

Turkey is agriculturally, abundantly productive, one of seven nations in the world totally self-sufficient and able to export food in quantity. As they automate their agriculture and develop more efficient farming and irrigation systems they will become more valuable in a hungry world. Seeing the women bent over weeding and planting by hand, and still knowing how abundant the produce is, one realizes the world must take this country seriously. I have never seen outdoor markets, in towns such as Bodrum, equal in variety and quality and certainly in price. We ate deliciously in Turkey.

One aspect of visiting Turkey we did not like was the aggressive way the merchants in tourist centers approached their potential clients. In towns like Marmarus, tourism is newly developed. Merchants have had little experience with good and bad cycles so the Gulf War, and its subsequent affect on tourism, has the merchants scrambling for the available tourist dollars. There were rows of leather, rug, gift, and jewelry shops, each with someone outside ready to force you in to look at their wares. It became a challenge, to simply walk down a street.

In addition to all the resort building, all the larger towns are building huge marinas. Some of them are absolutely beautiful with every facility one could wish, but with price tags geared to two week chartered yacht vacationers going back to a paying jobs, not the penny pinching long term cruisers like us. Luckily, we were able to find plenty of places to anchor without going into a marina. Some of these anchorages were beautiful, especially between Kemer and Finike. The steep cliff-sided inlets covered with fragrant pine trees and goatherds were a delight to the eye. The water in the Mediterranean in general, but especially in Greece and Turkey is crystal clear. Unfortunately, there is little to see below the surface. There are very few fish as the Med has been over fished for centuries and of course, no coral. In places where there are ruins of ancient cities you are not allowed to swim. The clear water does, however, make anchoring easier, as so much of the bottom is weed covered. On occasion we hunted anchorages for hours in order to place the anchor securely in one small available patch of sand. Consequently, the Mediterranean plague of anchor dragging has seldom been a problem for us. Once you have weed in your anchor you have no choice but to take it up, pick out the entire tangle of weed, and start over

We slowly day sailed our way up the West Coast of Turkey as far as Bodrum before crossing to Kos, our first Greek port. Because of the not too cordial relations between Turkey and Greece you cannot jump back and forth between the two countries, which would be convenient in the Greek Islands. Many are within a few hours of the Turkish coast. This cruise has been a tremendous lesson in geography. I never realized there were so many Greek Islands. It gives and understand to the term 'Greek shipping tycoon' when you see the vast amount of inter island traffic. A sharp lookout is required at all times. Our preconception of Turkey and Greece, as far as numbers of charter boats, was totally wrong. We expected Greece to be congested, but it was Turkey that was crowded with flotillas, bare boat charters, and a type of huge wooden sailing vessel, indigenous to the area. The latter have masts, occasionally with sails, but are mainly driven by massively powerful diesels. They are beautifully built and carry about 10 or 12 passengers on day sails or weeklong cruises. There are hundreds of them in each of the larger harbors and it was rare to find an anchorage without several. They anchor Med style with an anchor off the bow, and the stern tied to shore. We prefer to swing on one anchor, but must follow the accepted local way of doing things. It does allow many more yachts to share a crowded anchorage. With a folding prop and our inability to reverse efficiently creates some tense moments. One of these resulted in my getting very painful rope burns on my hand. Silvadine Cream saved a great deal more pain and quickened healing. I recommend it be included in any first aid kit.

In the short Mediterranean cruising season mid April to mid October, it would be difficult to visit all of the anchorages and harbors and islands of western Turkey and Greece. We were determined to get as much of a sample as possible in the short time we had. In talking with our Greek cruising friend Mark had found out a lot about the characteristics of the various island groups and they had marked on our charts the places which were most interesting, or had something out of the ordinary. It kept us on the move the whole time, but it was worth it. I won't go into a day-by-day chronicle, but try to tell you of the areas I found particularly interesting.

It is difficult to believe that the Turks occupied almost all of the Greek Islands in the Aegean for 4 to 5 hundred years and the Greeks and Turks remained totally separated until you realize the Turks are Muslim and the Greeks Christian. The islands closest to the coast of Turkey have the most churches and shrines and chapels. The Greek Church actually owns one island, Patmos. Although you may visit and tour through parts of the seminary/fort on the hilltop, you are required to dress appropriately. In case you are not prepared, skirts and long trousers are available at the entrance. There are no discos or noisy cafes although the town does cater, quietly, to tourists. Patmos is also the supposed site of the cave where St. John wrote the book of Revelations, and it is now a chapel.

The Greeks are so much more relaxed towards tourism than the Turks, but perhaps that is because they have experienced it for a longer time. They are used to the cycle of good years as well as down times. You can get what you want in their shops, but don't feel harassed if you are only window-shopping.

Mytilini, on the island of Lesvos is not a tourist town. Other places on the island are. Mytilini is a town with few charms unless you want to see a real Greek town inhabited by merchants, farmers and small factory workers. We put our bicycles ashore and spent three days exploring the town and the countryside.

If you look at a map of the Aegean, up at the top northwest corner there is a peninsula with three fingers extending southeast. This is the Kalkidhiki peninsula and the eastern most of the fingers totally fascinated me. The Aptos peninsula, with Mt. Athos towering 6,670 feet. The Greek Church governs the entire peninsula. The inhabitants of the peninsula are monks, hermits and holy scholars and there are about 25 immense monasteries dating back to the 9th century. Women are forbidden to set foot on the peninsula and yachts with women aboard may not anchor. The day we sailed past the peninsula, we had light winds and clear visibility so we were able to view the magnificent architecture and the modest hermit caves with our binoculars. Some of the monasteries are perched on the side of Mt. Athos so precariously one wonders how they have survived so many centuries in this earthquake prone country. The largest housed as many as 6000 men and it is only one of many. The population varies by century, and is slightly down at the moment. In centuries when the Church has been in danger the population has increased. It is this concentration of religious houses that preserved the culture and religion of Greece through the Dark Ages. There are no roads in. All traffic is by donkey or by ship and although a couple of the monasteries closest to the mainland have electricity, the rest do not. Inland it is a wild country where jackals are heard at night. The prevailing winds, which thankfully were not blowing the day we were there, usually whip down Mt. Athos gusting to at least 50 making the hermit caves seem uninhabitable, particularly in winter, but they are there and there are plenty of them.

From here we headed south to the Sporades, and what I thought was one of the prettiest towns in Greece, Skopelos. It is the sort of a town featured in post cards of Greek Islands. Geraniums filled every window box. There were tiny twisty lanes, wide enough for donkeys. Whitewashed buildings with bright blue trim decorated the hills, and of course, an abundance of lovely churches. A truly delightful place. From here on sailing downwind through the Cyclades we were grateful for the advice of our Greek friend. This area feels the strongest of the summer Meltimi winds. These winds frequently reach gale force, especially at headlands and funneling between the islands. We frequently had far more wind than we wanted, even though we were sailing downwind.

We had to go to Mykinos to pick up mail, and it was sort of fun, being the tourist center of the tourist filled Cyclades. It is located at the heart of the Meltimi slot. We were anchored on the lee side of the island, with two anchors, out and had to put on our foul weather jackets to get ashore in the dingy it was so choppy. In spite of all the heavy winds we encountered in the Med we still motored a higher proportion of the time than we had anywhere else thus far in our trip. Either it was too windy or calm—very little in between.

Anchored within a ferry ride of Piraeus, the port serving Athens, Mark went off for a day to attempt to replace some boat bits. He was about 50% successful, which, considering the language difference was excellent. For boats in a hurry to get to the Ionian, the Corinth Canal, for a healthy fee, offers a short cut, but we took the scenic route around the bottom of the Pelopisias, and on up to the islands of the Ionian Sea. These islands are much different than the Aegean. The architectural style is more Italian, and the plethora of church, chapels, and shrines diminishes, perhaps because they were not forced to defend their faith in this area as they had to facing Turkey.

I haven't mentioned castles, forts and ruins because they are everywhere and I could not describe them all in a letter. Even the smallest town has some sort of a ruin and that is what we spent our time doing in Turkey or Greece. Climbing over, hiking around, photographing and exploring antiquities. There are of course the famous sites, such as Delphi, Delos, Ephesus, but these usually involve entrance fees and guides. With a good general guidebook, to give you an overview of the history, you can find your own way and enjoy the off-the-beaten track places less frequented and less accessible.

We had obtained copies of all the cruising guides for the Med when we were in Cypress and the more Mark studied them, and the more we spoke to cruisers who had spent time in Spain, France and Italy, the more we came to realize it was not for us. The cost of living in Turkey and Greece was within our budget, and allowed us to eat well and occasionally eat ashore, but the cost as you move west, skyrockets. The coast of Italy is very smooth and therefore, almost all the harbors are man made. In France and Spain, the sheer number of yachts and marinas means most of the well-protected anchorages have already been taken for permanent marinas or moorings. Those remaining are exposed and listed as day-anchorage only. Mark was never crazy about the idea of leaving the boat in Cypress and going home to try to obtain temporary employment. So, we finally decided to make a quick trip to Gibraltar, haul out and do the bottom (not having done it in two years) and head across the Atlantic this year.

After a few weeks' in the lovely Ionian Islands, with their moderate breezes and green hills, we checked out of Greece, bound west. We passed through the straight of Messina with light winds and no whirlpools. We kept going until we reached Sardinia, where we spent about a week, day sailing and waiting out some horrible thunderstorms. We explored and loved Bonifacio, the spectacular walled city on the south coast of Corsica, then sailed to the Spanish Balearic Islands,

Minorca, Mallorca and Ibiza where we spent about ten days. We then sailed directly to Gibraltar. The cruising guides were right about the lack of secure anchorages and crowded marinas and the folks we had spoken to right about the cost. After the sample of the western Med we had tasted we were glad we had decided not to try to spend another season. Perhaps, for retired folks, with good pensions, the western Med would be a delightful place to spend time, but not for us right now. Swimming in a quiet lagoon with fish below, no tourists and an occasional yachtie for company, is still our ideal cruising, not marina hopping.

The winter comes early to the western Med. The north Atlantic fronts come roaring through as early as mid September and the weather deteriorates rapidly. We had gale force winds twice between Italy and Gibraltar and the thing I fear most, fierce lightening storms.

I won't be sorry to leave the Med from a sailing point of view, although I loved the scenery, history, and wonderful food. Now, however, the trade winds beckon. Will write again. Best wishes for the Holiday Season. Hoping to hear from you.

Laraine Salmon

Letter 11
Gibraltar to Panama

Gibraltar, the Rock, stood ahead looking like an immense Prudential Insurance advert. As I have said so often before, "nothing ever seems to be as one expects." Somehow, I expected the British stronghold, guarding the entrance to the Mediterranean, to be much larger. In reality the actual area is probably no more than three miles long and a half a mile wide. The Rock however is impressive and dominates the landscape. I guess, at one time, it dropped straight into the sea, but landfill has extended the area and now includes an airport, which although not large, provides considerable entertainment for those anchored next to it. Flights are infrequent, and the runway stretching far out into the bay is a delightful resting-place for the huge flocks of seagulls in the area. Before an aircraft is scheduled to land or take off an airport employee drives down the runway in a little van and sets off firecrackers to scare away the birds. They protect bitterly, but fly off only to return once the noise and confusion and the landing of the plane are over.

The boat had not been hauled out of the water for two years, since New Zealand, so Gibraltar's Yacht Harbor became its home for several weeks. Mark did a wonderful job making Arietta shine, polishing the topsides, repainting the name and stripe, polishing all the fittings as well as doing the bottom. It looked like a totally new boat when he was done. Meanwhile, I flew home at the request of my parents. My mother was having surgery for cancer. Not the ideal reason for a visit, but even so, I was glad to see them after so long.

We departed Gibraltar Dec 1 bound for the Canary Islands. The weather report appeared to be good so we expected to arrive in 5 or 6 days. Unfortunately most weather reports are only good for about 3 days. We were just about half way when a serious low caught us and we were clobbered by a nasty Atlantic storm. We heard later that it was the worst to hit the Canary Islands in seventy years and caused major damage to ports on the south shore of several Islands. We were too close to the African coast for comfort, but the winds were at first from the east, so we ran with them. They gradually turned more southerly and we ended up being blown three hundred miles northwest. At times we were pegging the knot meter at 10 knots with bare poles so, to make steering easier for the Aries we put out a loop of 300 feet of ¾ inch line. This helped considerably. It was a frightening experience. The storm lasted three days and during that time we never saw less than 45 knots and frequently 55–60. At one-point waves breaking over the transom forced water into the exhaust. It happened in spite of a rather complicated looping system meant to prevent this very problem. We found ourselves having to change the engine oil in 45 knots of wind, which, as you can well imagine, produced monstrous seas. Luckily, neither of us is particularly prone to seasickness. Finally the storm blew itself out and we were able to head south again. Instead of the 5–6 days we anticipated for this passage, it was almost 12 when we finally arrived in Tenerife, tired, but in one piece.

Our stay was very brief. We had to dry out, tidy up a bit, do laundry and reprovision. I would have like to stay longer, but it was getting to be winter and we did not want to be this far north for too much longer. We spent Christmas and New Years at sea between the Canary Islands and Antigua our first stop in the Caribbean. Having the ham radio has been useful on many occasions, but being able to call my parents Christmas morning was especially wonderful.

Antigua, from the Canary Islands, took 20 days. Not a record, but not too bad either. English Harbor and the Nelson Dockyard are Antiguan historic restoration areas and one feels as though you are anchored in the middle of a postcard. Folks coming by land must pay an entrance feel to enter and yachts pay an anchoring fee, but the setting is lovely and the anchorage well protected. We met up with friends from Gibraltar and the Canaries and had a great time. Mark, although a tremendous swimmer, free diving easily to 30 feet (we try to anchor in 30 feet or less) had never done any scuba diving, so in Antigua he took a course and became a certified diver. He later rented equipment a couple of times but decided he preferred snorkeling for its quiet unencumbered feeling. From Antigua we sailed to Guadeloupe a day sail away. The French islands we visited certainly had a different atmosphere from the independent islands. The French islands are more prosperous, and sophisticated. Probably, as in French Polynesia, the local economy is heavily subsidized and boosted by trade with France. Port-a-Pitre the main center is historically interesting and quite attractive. The Saints, small islands south of Guadeloupe were particularly charming, one of our favorite spots in the Windward Islands.

We stopped very briefly in Dominica and in Martinique a good place to stock up on French wines. On St Lucia we met up with friends we met in the Marquesas over three years ago and cruised with through Indonesia and up the Red Sea.

They were on their way home to North Caroline, so we had to say a final, sad farewell to "Flying Dolphin."

With brief stops in St Vincent, the Grenadines and Grenada we completed our quick trip through the heavily cruised, windy Windward Islands. Unfortunately we had set ourselves a target date for getting back to California, and still had a lot of miles to cover. Isle de Margarita, belonging to Venezuela was an excellent provisioning port as long as you purchased non-imported items. The shopping was very economical for those exchanging US currency, but for local people the inflation is dreadful, and the stability of the government rather shaky.

The next three islands, Venezuelan owned, were our favorite stops in the Caribbean. Blanquilla, Los Roques and especially Las Aves were sparsely populated had less crowded anchorages and better snorkeling than we had seen thus for in the Caribbean.

One shocking feature, to me at least, was how the conch has been hunted to near extinction throughout the Caribbean. We saw places where there were huge towering hills of conch shells along the beach and it was rare to see even small ones alive in the water. They are hunted commercially and in parts of the Netherlands Antilles have become an endangered species, and are now a protected species.

The three Dutch islands, Bonaire, Curacao and Aruba referred to, as the ABC islands, were surprisingly dry and barren. They are appealing to tourists for their beaches, casinos and diving. Mark went for a dive here and enjoyed it but said the interesting parts were quite deep and at snorkel depth there was little to see. As a non-diver I was disappointed that an area so famous for diving did not have good snorkeling as well.

Spanish Waters Bay in Curacao is one of the best natural harbors we've visited. A tiny entrance opens up into multiple fingers of water with well-protected, attractive anchorages. The most popular is near Sarafundie. This private "yacht club" is unique in many ways. It is an open air, on the water, house with a huge dingy dock. The couple that own and operate it charge a modest weekly fee for use of the facilities. Everything is done on the honor system. You can help yourself to beer, wine, soft drinks and snacks or even take a shower and mark it down on a list posted by the bar. You can do laundry, or twice a week hop on their van for a ride to the supermarkets. On Friday, everyone is expected to pay. It seems to work, and what is nice is that the prices are fair. Mark spent two weeks here while I went home to see my folks. Mom was in the hospital again.

From Curacao we intended to go to the Panamanian San Blas Islands but due to an unpleasant weather report stopped briefly in Aruba. The area north of the

Columbia/Venezuela border is notorious for it seas. There is a knot of westerly current, which swings south at Panama, then follows the land contours and ends up bumping back into itself causing the seas to become very steep for about 150 miles. The heavier the wind the worse it is so you try to get a favorable weather report, and we did. Naturally after two days it changed and the wind increased.

It wasn't actually too much wind for a pleasant downwind sail—perhaps 30–35, but the seas were getting huge. With two people it is impossible to hand steer 24 hours a day for days or weeks at a time. We have an Aries wind operated steering device that has seen us through a lot of different conditions safely, but these seas were just too much for it. We came off one wave sideways and the next rolled us on our side. It could have been worse. At least neither of us was in the cockpit at the time it happened, or we probably would not be here to tell about it. The top of the mast must not have hit the water because none of the instruments or antenna were damaged but it did do damage on deck and in the cabin. After that one wave the Aries got control and we sailed on with no other incidents but did partially hand steer for about the next eight hours until the seas subsided some-what.

The damage from that one wave was more than in the Tasman Sea or between Gibraltar and the Canaries. The dodger was in shreds, the awning was completely gone and the stern pulpit had come out of its base fitting in two places. One stan-chion was broken at the base, and three cushions and our waterproof flashlight were gone. The wind had been strong enough all along so we had never put up the Mainsail, just the jib. The force of the water over the boat had ripped off all the fasteners on the main sail cover. Inside the boat was a mess. The contents of the galley had emptied and landed in the chart table area saturating some of the navigation books with broken bottles of vanilla, chutney, Worcestershire, garlic, marjoram etc. A potent mix! Mark had been safe in his bunk and I was sitting on the settee, which became the low side, so I was not thrown across the cabin. We had a case of soda in the pilot berth across from me and it flew over my head and landed in the opposite pilot berth fortunately without hitting me. Dishes were broken and chipped and worst of all, even though the hatch had been closed, enough water had been forced though to stop the ham radio from working.

The rest of the trip to the San Blas Islands was uneventful and the wind grad-ually dropped until we had to motor the last couple of miles into the anchorage. We spent a week cleaning up, re-stitching and patching the dodger and trying to relax a bit. These islands were the perfect place to do it. They are tiny coral islands with palm trees, white sand beaches and turquoise lagoons. The Cuna Indians who live here are tiny people. At five foot, one inch height I towered over them and Mark looked like a giant. The women sew reverse applique pictures or patterns traditional and modern, called molas. They sell them and the men sell their fish and crayfish. That appears to be their whole life and livelihood. Most islands are without any electricity. The houses are thatch roofed, perfect for the gentle climate and their boats, both sail and paddle, are dugouts. They are gentle, friendly people and I was delighted to purchase several molas. At some time another cruiser must have given them a Walt Disney picture book because one of the ones I purchased was of the character Dumbo the flying elephant. They all had the tiniest hand stitching I've ever seen and the brilliant colors are a joy to behold—a treasure for me to keep, as a reminder of this peaceful place and it's tiny gentle people.

From here we sailed to Panama. We had a radio to repair and an awning to replace and the excitement of the Panama Canal transit to anticipate.

Bye for now

Love to all, Laraine

Letter 12
Panama to California

Panama is a very poor country with a lot of problems. The first thing you are told when you check into the Panama Yacht Club is not to walk to town alone. The Yacht Club is very secure with guards and tall fences but once outside your safest mode of transportation is a taxi. There is a great deal of paper work involved in going through the canal but not so much that you need to hire an agent. While we were there they had a large anti government protest, which would not have been a problem, except that it blocked the road between the Yacht Club and the supermarket. You must have four line handlers, a helmsman and the pilot onboard for the canal transit and are expected to feed them all, so I was a bit concerned about provisioning. Fortunately the protest lasted just one day so the next day I filled a cab with groceries for the trip. We had two Canadians, a couple traveling by land, who though it would be fun to transit the canal, and a Panamanian chap who had been raised in New York, so spoke English fluently. The pilot we were assigned was quite entertaining so we had a great trip. Depending on the start time it is possible to get through in one day. However we were delayed because of some sort of technical difficulties in one of the locks so it was late when we arrived in Goton Lake. There are three locks going up, a Lake and channel across the high country, then three locks down to the Pacific. The yachts are rafted three abreast and the day we went through there were a total of twelve yachts, which all easily fit into one lock. It was a lot of fun, not nearly as frightening as I expected. At the end of the day we enjoyed swimming in fresh water and scrubbing all the salt off the boat. Swimming in fresh water after nearly four years of swimming in salt water was strange. You felt as though rocks were tied to you feet, and you really had to work to stay afloat.

The next day we continued down to the Pacific where we tied up in the Balboa Yacht Club mooring area. Our crew departed and we picked up fresh groceries for the next trip. In a way it was unfortunate that Mark had managed to get the ham radio operating himself, after the knock down, so we didn't bother to take it to a repair shop. We were in the Perlas Islands when it quit completely, so we had to return to Balboa and find a Kenwood dealer. He repaired it, but there was a considerable delay in getting started again. All the other repairs had been completed in Colon.

From Panama we had a very slow windless, sometimes sail, sometimes motor, to Cocos Island. This is a Costa Rican Park. Never inhabited, except by park rangers and the occasional stranded, shipwrecked seamen, it is a beautiful, wonderland of jungles, waterfalls and fresh water pools. The amazing, delightful absence of biting bugs was a total joy for me. To be able to hike all day in a tropical rain forest and perhaps see one mosquito is heaven to a person who usually acts as a mosquito magnet. The anchorages are not wonderful, but the island was more than worth a bit of discomfort. From Cocos we planned to go to the Galapagos, but, due to unfavorable winds, tight schedule and mixed reviews from other yachts, decided to miss it this time. The problem with going there by private yacht is that you are only allowed to visit one place and if you want to travel to see the interesting areas you need to take a tour, a bit much for our already over stretched cruising budget.

The logical way to get from Panama to San Francisco is to sail up the coast of Central America and Mexico, but here we broke with tradition and logic and headed for the Marquesas. We had a slow start but once into the southwest trades we had some of the most consistent long runs of our trip. I was able to keep in close touch with my parents via ham radio, which was good, because it is a long way between telephones. It was 33 days from Panama to Nuke Hiva including stops along the Panama coast and Cocos Islands, but neither of them had a telephone. About half way to Nuka Hiva we debated as to whether we should go directly to Hawaii. The plans we had for visiting French Polynesia again had changed when we heard, via ham radio, that the people we hoped to visit in Toau were no longer there. The two yachts we hoped to rendezvous with, a reunion after three years, in Toau, where we met, had changed plans, one boat would not make it due to being dismasted. About this time, Mark developed a toothache. Again, via ham radio, we called home to a ham radio operator friend in our yacht club (Steve Salmon) and he put us in touch with a dentist. The dentist suggested antibiotics, which we had onboard and pain pills, as needed. Since Nuka Hiva was closer than Hawaii we headed there. By the time we arrived the toothache had fortunately disappeared since the only dentist was on a two-month vacation.

We stayed there just long enough to restock and do a few minor repairs before heading north to Hawaii. Because we were there for such a brief time we were not required to pay the bond. The French officials were pleasant and stamped us in and out with no fuss. On the trip to Hawaii I recovered from all the No No and mosquito bites. They are the only thing preventing the Marquesas from being a tropical paradise, but probably help to keep the islands free of too much tourist development.

The area north of Nuka Hiva, is a good place to cross the ITCZ (inter tropic convergence zone) also referred to as the Doldrums. The squalls are less frequent and the distance across usually narrower than areas farther east or west. We encountered no electrical storms at all on this passage—Oh Joy.

Five days before I arrived in Hawaii my Mom passed away. We landed in Hilo July 1, and I flew home the next day. Mark began his first experience of single handling. He sailed from Hilo to Kahului the main town on the east of Maui then, Honolulu Bay a pretty cove on the north of Maui. From there, he sailed to Lono Harbor, a disused barge harbor on the rural, unpopulated ranching end of Molokai. From there, on to Kaneohe Bay, Oahu where he was just in time to meet the racing fleet arriving from San Francisco in the Pacific Cup Race. Many of the racers were friends from home. I flew back to Hawaii for two weeks to join him and we had a great time participating in the end of race festivities. This is a race I did in 1980 which was the very first Pacific Cup. When all the parties were over we sailed on to Kauai for a week of relaxing. We blew our cruising budget and rented a car, a must on Kauai, with no bus service available, and threw a picnic in the cooler every morning for our island exploring.

At that point, I came home and Dennis Murphy joined Mark for the trip to SF Bay. We had completed our circumnavigation before reaching Nuka Hiva and I wanted to spend some time enjoying my fathers delightful company while I had the chance. Mark had a reasonable trip back. Dennis hadn't done a great deal of ocean sailing but had dreams of going cruising. After the passage to S.F. he still felt the same, which was good.

Now we are back. Sort of a shock in many ways since quite a bit has changed in the four years we've been gone. Our priority right now is finding employment and getting back into the swing of life on land. We are ready to be back, especially from the financial standpoint. We have had a good time, collected memories that we will treasure for the rest of our life. And we've done something few people ever have the opportunity to do.

We have sailed around the world.

Hope to see you soon,

Love to all, Laraine

0-595-27972-4

Printed in the United States
1114500001B